TWO
HUNDRED
MILLION
AMERICANS
IN SEARCH OF
A GOVERNMENT

OTHER BOOKS
BY E. E. SCHATTSCHNEIDER

Politics, Pressures and the Tariff

Party Government

The Struggle for Party Government

A Guide to the Study of Public Affairs
(with Victor Jones and Stephen K. Bailey)

The Semisovereign People: A Realist's View of Democracy
in America

TWO
HUNDRED
MILLION
AMERICANS
IN SEARCH OF
A GOVERNMENT

E. E. Schattschneider

HOLT, RINEHART AND WINSTON, INC.
New York   Chicago   San Francisco   Atlanta
Dallas   Montreal   Toronto   London   Sydney

204964

PREFACE

It is extremely unlikely that the prehistoric founders of primitive governments were sufficiently interested in political theory to feel a need to define the institutions they created. They were far too busy fighting for survival to think about sovereignty, obedience, and democracy. Several thousand years later, when philosophers began to speculate about human affairs, government was taken for granted, treated as a work of nature. Perhaps these circumstances account for the general absentmindedness with which political scientists have passed over the problem of defining government.

This book argues that it is bad philosophy, poor scholarship, and reckless political practice to become as greatly involved with government as we are today without making an effort to find out what it is.

Historically, many figures and images have been used to explain government (crowns, thrones, scepters, purple robes, bits of bunting, lions, dragons, and eagles). To these the author has added a few of his own—two versions of a parlor game, the crew of a ship at sea in a storm, a raft, a football game in which all of the players are on one side, a one-man baseball game, a hole (the hole in political theory), and an oyster. Perhaps these new images will do something to remind political scientists of a forgotten problem.

Chapters 1, 2, and 7 deal with the hard shell of the oyster, while chapters 3, 4, 5, and 6 deal with the soft inside. Obviously the inside and the outside of the oyster are so closely related that the whole book is about the search of the two hundred million for a government.

The author is grateful to Arlene Beckley who, many years ago, gave him a copy of Walker's A *Critical Pronouncing*

v

Dictionary and Expositor of the English Language, and to Anne Crescimanno, who typed and retyped the manuscript through many revisions with the patience of a saint.

Old Saybrook, Conn.   **E. E. S.**
July 1969

CONTENTS

Preface   v

CHAPTER *1*
What are we looking for?   3

CHAPTER *2*
*Why do people make miscalculations about
    government?*   27

CHAPTER *3*
Democracy as a moral system   41

CHAPTER *4*
Democracy as a form of government   57

CHAPTER *5*
*Why is a generation the proper period of time
    for the study of politics?*   81

CHAPTER *6*
Some political words   99

CHAPTER *7*
*Some nongovernmental thoughts about the future of
    government*   115

Appendix   123

Index   131

But how I caught it, found it, came by it,
What stuff 'tis made of, whereof it is born,
I am to learn.

—*The Merchant of Venice*

CHAPTER *1*

What are we looking for?

In the folklore of government, every American is born free and equal, and a little know-it-all as far as a government is concerned. Little children learn to count, they learn to spell, and they learn that 2 + 2 is 4, but nobody tells them what government is; they already know. Nobody tells anybody what government is. Nobody learns what it is. Nobody asks. The answer is not in the books, and it is impossible to find anyone who can remember when he did not know.

That is how we begin the study of government—in the worst possible way.

Nevertheless, anyone who takes the trouble to ask some foolish questions is likely to find some confusion about the subject. What kinds of *images* do people have in mind when they think about government? When they are pinned down, it turns out that they have a variety of pictures in mind. Some people associate it with a piece of bunting or a bit of parchment, a place, a building, a person, a relic, or a seal. Other people in other times have identified government with a piece of headgear, a chair, a robe, a lion, an eagle, a cock, a wand, a hammer and sickle, a star, or a weapon. Sometimes they personify 'government as Uncle Sam or John Bull or the figure of a woman or a monster, a Leviathan, a Behemoth, or a dragon. Perhaps more often nowadays they imagine that government is a *machine* or a *thing*.

Obviously, the personifications, images, and figures of speech that we use to visualize government suggest that we do not really know what it is. Has anyone ever seen a government or touched one? What is it made of? Even more important, what is the *cause* of government? Where do governments come from? Could we make one of our own if we wanted to? How did we get involved with government? Why do we obey the government? Where did governments get their power?

Wouldn't it be funny if it turned out that government is not what we think it is?

What makes it even funnier is that Americans *swallow the governmental proposition whole*, paradoxes, contradictions, puzzles, mysteries, and all. By logical processes nobody understands they take it, lock, stock, and barrel, and believe in it more than they believe in almost anything else.

Americans are not the only people who believe in government without knowing what it is. Nearly everybody else in the world does the same thing. The demand for government is overwhelming and universal. Of the 3.5 billion people in the world only a handful are outside the governmental system. That makes government the most universal human institution, and makes it the most successful idea in the world. Moreover, people believe in it with surpassing intensity. More people have died in defense of their governments than have died for any other cause in the world; governments are nearly the only organizations in the world for which people do die. Anarchism is to government what atheism is to religion, but in the world today there may be a million times as many atheists as there are anarchists. Anarchism is one of the least successful political movements on earth; its impact on the growth, strength, and universalization of government has been substantially zero. Never, apparently, have so many people believed so much in something they have understood so little.

The American quest for government began before there was an America, before there were any Americans. No settlement in the New World dared face the wilderness without a government. Long before anyone thought of uniting the settlements into a nation, the colonists had already become prolific breeders of governments—using royal patents and charters, imposed or extracted, compacts, or fundamental orders; they improvised governments, sometimes of dubious legality, no matter where or how. Americans produced governments wherever they went. No other people in the history of the world has written as many fundamental laws.

The question is: what have we been looking for? Our whole fantastic experience with government might have been happier and more successful had we had a better idea of what we wanted.

It is small wonder that government has been a controversial subject. It is easy to prove that anarchists do not know what government is, but what about the rest of us? Philosophers have beguiled us with tales about the origin of government about as convincing as the fables we tell children about where babies come from. Everybody has made miscalculations about government—nationalists, individualists, pacifists, internationalists, militarists, Marxists, imperialists, fascists, and royalists—none of them has gotten what he wanted. Is it possible that all of these miscalculations have something to do with the fact that people have neglected to find out what they are looking for?

In spite of the confusion, and all of the nonsense about the subject, government is much too remarkable to be left unexplained. There is nothing else like it, and we can hardly imagine a world without governments. Perhaps we ought to try to understand it.

So we are left with some questions.

What is the *cause* of government?

What makes it universal?

Why is government able to do things that no one else can do?

How did governments get into their dominant position
in the world?
What makes government possible?
Why have governments survived all disasters, all revolutions, all social and economic changes, and all
confusion?

Governments are the most powerful, the richest, most
universal organizations in the world, with more prestige and
greater resources than any other kind of organization; their hold
on the loyalty and imagination of people is incomparable. How
can we explain this development?

Why have all attempts to abolish government failed?
Governments have been overthrown but never abolished; anyone who overthrows a government is very apt to become a
government. Where do governments get the strength to persist?
Why have governments grown in power and wealth and prestige
in spite of all the complaints about their costs and burdens and
all of the controversies about them?

Abolishing government is not easy. As a matter of fact
government is just about the most difficult thing in all the world
to get rid of, so difficult that there seems to be no serious attempt
to abolish government going on anywhere in the world today.
None of the great cleavages in the world are about attempts to
get rid of government; there is no great conflict between people
who want to have governments and people who do not want
them. Conflicts about communism, race, religion, poverty,
imperialism, or democracy all assume a great role for government. All are based on some kind of dissatisfaction with government, all propose to modify the system, but none seeks to abolish
it. And pacifists almost never advocate anarchism as a way of
abolishing war, though only governments make war.

If we examine these controversies closely we are likely to
find that all go back to questions about the nature of government. What is the matter with the concepts of government on
which these controversies are based?

In this respect the revolutionists are as remarkable as the
anarchists in Spain who fought heroically to preserve the Spanish
republic. People who overthrow governments are amazingly

eager to perpetuate government. There have been many revolutions but few interregnums because the revolutionaries seem to have an irresistible impulse to govern. Perhaps as many as 90 percent of the people of the world today have overthrown their governments in the past fifty years, but *there are no vacancies.* Government occupies the whole inhabitable area of the earth because government, like nature, abhors a vacuum. According to J. David Bowen, the 1952 revolution in Bolivia was the 179th in Bolivian history, but after all of these revolutions, Bolivia still has a government.[1]

Thus, in spite of all criticisms of the political system and despite all attempts to change it, in spite of all revolutions and all disorders, government is still the most successful idea in the world. There is something very strange about the way people think about governments.

When we turn from the folklore of government to scholars and philosophers, we find that they too assume that everybody knows what government is, an assumption that has conditioned everything that they say about the subject. Nobody seems to be aware of this hole in political theory. Since a definition is a way of seeing things, what do scholars see when they look at government? We are in the strange position of having collected a vast quantity of data about government without having made a serious attempt to find out what it is.

Some typical definitions of government by political scientists (neither better nor worse than the others) will illustrate the point.

One scholarly work lists two definitions: (1) government is the act or fact of governing, and (2) government is a mode or system of governing. Another skirts the problem by saying that government is "the official, legally sanctioned activities of legislators, judges, executive and administrative officials and public employees who carry on the work that is called government."

Still another textbook takes it for granted that everybody knows what government is and continues for a thousand pages without telling us what it is.

[1] J. David Bowen, "Bolivia's Revolution Comes of Age," *The Reporter,* September 26, 1963.

The *Encyclopaedia Brittanica* glides past the problem and begins by classifying governments. To say the least, *Brittanica* displays an overwhelming lack of curiosity about the subject. The reader can make his own collection of definitions, semi-definitions and circumlocutions by which men of learning have tried to evade the question. What the scholars and philosophers are giving us is a circular definition—a government is something that governs, or a government is a government, is a government, is a government. All of which proves that scholars are about as culturebound as is the man in the street.

In the literature of political science and political theory there is no serious theory of the formation of governments or the cause of government. For all we can read in the works on political theory, we might suppose that people are able to make any kind of government that meets their fancy, much as they might get together with their friends to form a club. The successful management of public affairs calls for a better insight.

There is nothing wrong about studying an unknown subject, but it is bad to begin by assuming that we already know what it is without having inquired. Political science is something of a shambles because scholars start with an assumption that precludes questions about the gist of the subject. Nearly all great problems in political science are related to some concept of what government is—whether political scientists know it or not, nearly everything that they think turns about the unasked question.

This is the first question: this is where political science begins. Even if we do not know what it is, this is where we start because we are not likely to get anywhere until we have some kind of answer, even if it is only a hypothesis to be tested.

There is something strange about the feeling of scholars that a definition is not necessary. Inevitably there is a lack of focus in the discipline because it is difficult to see things that are undefined. People who cannot define the object of their studies do not know what they are looking for, and if they do not know what they are looking for, how can they tell when they have found it?[2] How can we understand the data unless we relate them to something larger?

[2] Political science: a mountain of data surrounding a vacuum.

We might begin by trying to find out what makes government possible at all. Can anyone be said to know anything about government until he can answer that question? How is it done? People have known for a long time that birds can fly, but *man* had to find out how it was done before *he* could fly.

Thus we come to the *pons asinorum* of political science: how does one prove that government is possible at all? Why do 200 million Americans obey their government or 3.5 billion people obey a hundred governments? It is not fully satisfactory to say that a hundred governments exist and therefore we know that government is possible. How is it done?

There is something about government that demands an explanation, and if we cannot find the answer we ought to stop pretending that we understand the subject.

Government is often defined in terms that make it seem impossible, or that lead us to underestimate its strength or lead us to attribute its strength to the wrong cause. What we need is a reasonable explanation of how it is done. If we cannot find an answer to this question, nothing else we say about government is likely to make sense. How is it possible to govern 200 million people, or even one million or a thousand or ten? Would we not be able to do a better job of it if we knew?

Since the problem is an unfamiliar one we might try to arrange our thoughts by working on a simple hypothetical case, an exercise in which we break the job down into its component parts. What can we do with the A, B, C's of the problem? Merely for the fun of it we might make up a game—call it *Plato* or *Leviathan* or *Sovereignty*. Toying with the idea, how would you go about it to make a very small government of your own? You might invite ten friends, your putative subjects, to a party. You could hardly tell them in advance about your plan because they would not come if they knew what you were going to do to them. How would you subjugate them? You might take them one at a time, starting by overpowering a small friend. Assuming that you are able to wrestle him to the floor, what would you do with him? Tie him up? He would not like it; besides, what good will a tied-up ex-friend do you? Your guests will certainly be astonished at your conduct!

Continuing the experiment, you might, if you are very strong, tie up two or three other guests but probably no more because the others are likely to stop you; there will be a great change in the climate of the party as you proceed with your plan. No man is as strong as ten, and difficulties mount as you proceed. Overpowering people is hard and dangerous work, but it is only the beginning. What do you do with your new, very reluctant subjects? Suppose that after superhuman exertions you get them locked up. What then? Would you feed them or let them starve? If you decide to feed them you might have to spend the rest of your life supporting them, a strange way to acquire ten dependents. Moreover, once you have gone that far it would be dangerous to release them. You might kill your subjects, but what good will ten dead men be to you? No matter how you play that game, the odds are against you.

The game is a silly one, but it ought to teach us that *it is impossible to win the game as it was set up in the project.* Moreover, the image of government on which the game is based is as bad as the game. A surprising number of people have been hung up on this point of infeasibility!

Is there another way to set up the game? We can change everything by changing conditions on the *outside* of the house. Let us imagine that your house is surrounded by a hostile mob trying to break down your doors, threatening to lynch you and your friends. Now you can take charge. It is easy to imagine that your friends would eagerly follow your directions, because you now have a new kind of relation with them. The tension is no longer between you and your friends but between the people inside the house and the people on the outside. Your friends *want* to be told what to do. In taking charge you do not alienate them. Indeed, if you survive, everyone in the house will be your friend for life.

The difference between the two games is total.

In changing the game we have also changed the image of government. In the first image we think of government in terms of a master and servant relation between the ruler and his subjects. The pattern of authority in the second game is like that of the crew of a ship at sea in a storm; all get into port together or all go down together. Everything depends on how we see government.

The trick is to get the people and the government on the same side.

The two ways of playing the parlor game are related to two ways of seeing government. One way to see government is to look at one government at a time. In this way we isolate a government, ignore everything else, and examine it as something complete in itself. This is the *introverted* way of looking at government, the classical way of seeing it, used by philosophers and scholars since Plato.

Looking at government this way forces us to think about government in terms of the relations between rulers and subjects, because the point of view excludes all other factors. When we ask ourselves why people obey, we cannot avoid saying that people obey because they are forced to do so. The introverted, keyhole way of looking at government is the logical base of the idea of government by force. Indeed, it is the mother of all illusions about government.

The notion that each government is a solitary and independent entity runs through the whole literature of politics. The worst thing about that notion is that we never find out what government is because it puts us on the wrong track. We fall into a kind of bottomless logical pit, just as we did in the first version of the parlor game.

As an isolated phenomenon a government seems to be something illogical. We cannot explain the origin or cause or growth or strength or universality of government because that introverted view of government has forced theorists to make the relations between rulers and subjects the focus of all political theory.

There is such a thing as getting too close to a subject to see it. Government is as large as the world; there ought to be an enlarged way of looking at it, a view that takes in the whole political landscape.

Everything we think about government is a matter of perspective. How does one go about it to see a government? The one-eyed, keyhole way of looking at government forces us to see one government at a time.

It forces us   ◯   one
to see this   government

Whereas   a multitude
we ought   of
to see this   governments

We ought to see a hundred governments, not one, because the impulse that makes governments comes from the outside.

The traditional view of government is all the more remarkable because no government has ever existed by itself. Our whole view of the dynamics of government, how it works, what makes it possible, the cause, depends on whether or not we understand that every government is surrounded by many other governments.

The question is: *why are there so many?* Governments are like bees, birds, fish, cattle, or wolves; they come in swarms, flocks, schools, herds, or packs, but never alone.

We begin to understand the subject when we realize that the multiplicity of governments is fundamental and crucial. The political organization of the world consists of a hundred governments in a state of tension.

The multiplicity of governments is no accident, because every government is an organization of a minority.

	FRACTION OF WORLD'S POPULATION
Afghanistan	1/250
Argentina	1/159
Belgium	1/388
Bolivia	1/1000
Brazil	1/46
Chile	1/437
China	1/5
Denmark	1/745
France	1/73
West Germany	1/63
India	1/8
Ireland	1/1160
Japan	1/36
USA	1/17
USSR	1/15
United Kingdom	1/66

We can turn these figures around to say that there are a thousand times as many people outside of Bolivia as there are inside, that the French are outnumbered 73 to 1. There are 3.3 billion people outside of the United States and almost as many outside of Russia, and the people on the outside have a great deal to do with the way the people on the inside feel. No matter how unified they may be at home, every nation is a minority in the world.

The nature of the government of the United States has a lot to do with the relations between the 200 million people on the *inside* of the country and the 3.3 billion people on the *outside*. It would be troublesome enough if the 3.3 billion people on the outside were merely people, but the trouble is multiplied tremendously by the fact that they are mobilized by a hundred governments. The logic of the situation suggests that governments are incurably minority organizations.

Governments are fantastically successful specialists in the organization of minorities. The perfect government may well be an organization of 1 percent of the world's population in the less than benevolent presence of the other 99 percent.

The political system of the world grows out of the fact that people are forced by the nature of things to live on the same planet with very large numbers of people whom they do not understand very well.[3] No matter how we look at them, all the people in the world are the cause of government. Government is about the condition of 3.5 billion people; what they think, how they feel. It is about the limitations and frailties of a vast number of human beings.

We start with a world full of *people who are afraid of each other*. No one has ever been able to cope with so great a multitude of people. No man has been able to cope intellectually with 3.5 billion people, to see or understand that many people. Understanding mankind is the greatest unsolved intellectual problem in the world.

It is not mere chance that no government has ever been able to govern the world, either by conquest or persuasion. Indeed, none of the governments in the world today are ever likely to be able to govern a majority of mankind,[4] and organizing a world government is a little like trying to play a football game in which all of the players are on one side.

Thus, what governments *can* do, defines what governments *cannot* do, and we come to the first law of political science: *the world is ungovernable*. It is necessary to have governments because the world is out of control.

One man alone among 3.5 billion people is bound to be frightened. This is the feeling on which government is based. As long as the total number of people in the world was small, widely scattered over large areas of the world, people could live on relatively easy terms with each other. If the total population of the earth had never exceeded a million, it is likely that no governments would ever have been formed.

As a matter of fact, it may be as good a guess as any that government originated in an ancient population explosion, perhaps about eight thousand years ago, when the invention of

[3] *The New York Times*, February 19, 1967, quotes a Chinese publication during the Sino-Russian crisis as saying to the Russians, "We won't live on one planet with you."
[4] It is likely that there would be something unstable about any government of two billion people.

farming in southwestern Asia greatly increased the food supply available to people. Farming, an increased food supply, a population explosion, the marriage of land and people, the exhaustion of soil by primitive farmers, and wars about the possession of land are the components out of which governments were made.[5]

In the history of man, the existence of a large population is something relatively new. In terms of a two million–year span, the growth of a large population on the earth has taken place in perhaps the last half of 1 percent of the time.[6]

What Jacquetta Hawkes says about the change in the way of life of primitive people between the early Neolithic period to the late Neolithic or early Bronze Age, perhaps eight or nine thousand years ago, is of great significance to students of government. Life in the early Neolithic age was peaceful. (Miss Hawkes notes the "general absence of weapons of war among the grave furniture of Neolithic burials.") On the other hand, in the late Neolithic and early Bronze Age "battle axes, daggers and other arms appear in the grave of every adult male."[7]

The evidence of the later development of war and government is overwhelming. The language used by archeologists tells us what was going on. Sir Leonard Wooley, describing life in the Bronze Age, uses words such as the following:[8]

garrison	royal family
armies	ruler
subjection	dynasts, dynasties
art of war	capital city
military power	small states
invaders	confederacy

[5] Robert Ardrey, in *The Territorial Imperative*, New York, 1966, contends that the attachment to the soil is prehuman in its origins. Perhaps we should say that farming intensified the attachment.

[6] "This vast increase in the number of human beings who could find livelihood on Earth, together with the tendency to exhaust soil, led to colonization of a number of localities, including many islands that had never been inhabited." Jacquetta Hawkes, *Prehistory*, New York, 1965, pp. 458–459.

[7] Hawkes, p. 358. See *The New York Times*, January 29, 1967, p. 6E, for a map of the spread of agriculture throughout the world. (See map in Hawkes, p. 326.)

[8] Sir Leonard Wooley, *The Beginnings of Civilization*, New York, 1963, pp. 49ff.

empire
independent state under a
    king
governments
war
princes
crowns
lords
enemy
warriors
capture
alien rule
nationalist resurgence
city states
overlords
petty kingdom
foreign conquest
inter-dynastic feuds
sovereignty
governors
rule
tyranny
official
stormed and sacked
coalition
allies
principalities
vassalage
confederacy
king
military tactics
corps d'elite
campaigning
surrender
envoys

interdynastic feuds
invasions
foreign tyranny
conquest
civil war
armed host
victory
power
ruling aristocracy
vanquished
alliance
royal marriage
peace
knights
chariotry
alien
fortified
mercenaries
weapons
arrows
spearheads
horsemen
walled city
ramparts
sea power
army of occupation
mercenaries
rebellion
ravaged, burned and slew
entrenched
raid
imperialistic venture
suzerainty
fortification
horsed chariot

buffer state
rebels
battle
occupation
imperialism
beleaguered
surrender
campaigning
armed invasion by
    foreigners
contour fort
stronghold
fortress housing royal
    troops
acropolis
inner walled city
lines of defense
outpost
old walled town
outer walls
citadels
sieze

raids
citizen levy
commander-in-chief
professional soldier
tribute
standing army
subdued
colony
walls
frontiers
tower great wall
prisoners of war
foreign recruits
foreign expeditions
trained officers
foreign mercenaries
military formation
phalanx
marching files
bow
conscription
ransom

Government today bears the marks of its origins. Like an oyster, it is hard on the outside and soft on the inside. We can now try to find the answer to the question raised in the *pons asinorum* of political science. Why do men obey? Is it true that governments rule principally by the use of force? The question of obedience deals with the nature of the soft inside of the governmental oyster.

There is something unsatisfactory about attempts to solve the riddle of government in terms of force, to identify government with force, or to say that the people obey governments only because they are forced to do so. That kind of analysis separates the government from the people and sets the government and the people in opposition to each other. To say that the government forces people to obey it merely raises a new question: *whose force does the government use?*

Whatever the relation of the people and the government may be, *force is on the side of the people.* Two hundred million Americans have all the force there is in the American community. The government of the United States is exceedingly powerful, but the power it uses is the power of people. Would it not be better to say that American government is an organization of the energy, intelligence, wealth, resources, and the productive capacity of the American people, because the government has no resources, money, energy, intelligence, courage, or integrity that it does not derive from the people?

It would be better to say that the government *is* the people; the government is the way people think and act. What does the American government consist of? It consists of the American people. The government is infinitely the most popular institution in the American community because it is really a form of community behavior.

What does the government of the United States look like? Look around at your family, friends, neighbors, and associates. That is what the government looks like because they *are* the government. Government by force does not fit into this way of looking at government.

The American government does use force, but it uses it *marginally* and *incidentally* and *externally* and does not characteristically use force to *govern.* It is an institution designed to mobilize the force of the people for common purposes.

The function of the police, for example, is not to govern a reluctant people by force but to protect the public against a lawless minority. In this case force is used in the service of nearly all of the people to restrain a chemical trace of outlaws, and consent and agreement are unstated conditions of its use. As a matter of fact, law enforcement is one of the most popular functions of the government; when the government curbs the outlaws it sometimes acts with an excess of public consent.[9]

---

[9] See what the *Report of the National Advisory Commission on Civil Disorders* (New York, 1968), has to say about the excessive use of force to put down riots in 1967. See Index p. 591.

The point is well illustrated by a comment once made by Clarence Darrow. He said, "If the American people were forced to choose between abolishing their schools, on the one hand, or abolishing their jails on the other hand, they would abolish their schools and keep their jails."

The great prestige of J. Edgar Hoover of the F.B.I. and the popularity of energetic prosecutors such as Thomas E. Dewey reflect this public attitude.[10] The bias of the public has been demonstrated in a multitude of polls and referenda.

The assumption of the legal system is that people very generally obey the law voluntarily. The limited capacity of American prisons, the limited capacity of the courts to try cases, and the limited number of police available show that the government is not organized to deal with large-scale resistance to the law. The dismal failure of the prohibition laws a generation ago shows how little government can do to cope with a general unwillingness to obey an unpopular law. Thus, public cooperation is a part of the calculation that goes into all legislation.

As a matter of fact, the force that the American government uses to police the country is a very small part of the force at its disposal. There are 316,000 national, state, and local law enforcement officials in the U.S.A., 90 percent local, while there are more than three million men in the armed forces, designed for use *outside* of the United States. The ratio ten to one does not show fully the predominance of force for external use. The defense budget of the United States is a hundred times as large as the law enforcement budget. In terms of the power and destructiveness of its weapons the American government is probably the most violent organization in the history of the world, but this violence is not designed to run the country. We cannot, for example, use the atomic bomb to govern the American people.

While there are about 300,000 persons in American prisons, there are about 200 million outside of prison. Only about 5 percent of all state and local government employees are police

---

[10] Mr. Dewey was prosecuting attorney in New York County, N.Y., later became governor of New York, and in 1948 was Republican presidential nominee.

officers. For the country as a whole, the number of persons in mental hospitals is three times as great as the prison population.

While about 8500 murders are committed in the U.S.A. annually, the odds against being murdered are very great. On the average an ordinary American might expect to live 23,000 years before he is murdered, and every year about 200 million Americans are *not* murdered. Why did 200 million Americans refrain from murdering each other? It is preposterous to suppose that they avoided killing each other because they were afraid of the government.

Prison architecture does not reflect a great fear of popular demonstrations against prisons, or a fear of violent attempts by the people at large to *release* prisoners. The public approves of prisons, approves of the punishment of offenders, and takes sides with the government against them.

Statistics concerning crime in the United States support the view that crime is rarely an attack on the government.

CRIMES COMMITTED IN 1958

Murder	8,182
Forcible rape	14,561
Robbery	75,347
Aggravated assault	113,530
Burglary	679,787
Larceny (over $50)	391,550
Auto theft	270,965

None of these offenses are seriously related to attempts to overthrow the government.

Thus, force used by the government within the United States is designed to protect the people against a lawless minority, and it is unlikely that the government is about to be overthrown by a combination of pickpockets, dope addicts, prostitutes, gamblers, vagrants, counterfeiters, shoplifters, or burglars. Offenses aimed at the *overthrow* of the government (sedition, treason, espionage, sabotage, and so on) amounted to a total of forty-two cases involving 132 defendants in 1959, and in any given year there are likely to be as many two-headed calves born in the United States as there are convicted traitors.[11] In view of the fact that the ratio of students in American schools and colleges to persons confined in prison is about 220 to 1, is it not more reasonable to say that the characteristic activity of American government is education rather than coercion?

The obsession with force has led many Americans into a distorted view of other activities of the government. One function of American government, almost wholly a state and local government function, is the regulation of motor vehicle traffic. A widespread press, radio, and television publicity campaign has created the impression that the "slaughter on the highways" has taken on the proportions of a national disaster. The illusory nature of this notion becomes evident as soon as we look at the statistics of highway deaths in relation to total highway traffic. In 1965 Americans traveled 1370 billion passenger miles in automobiles and taxis. The death rate was 2.4 per 100 million passenger miles. Since there are only about five full-time traffic officers for each ten thousand persons throughout the country, it is clear that 99 million licensed American automobile drivers were remarkably law abiding even though they are not closely supervised by the police.

Perhaps even more remarkable is the experience of the Federal Internal Revenue Service in the collection of the income tax. In 1964, more than 65 million tax returns were made, reporting 229 billion in taxable income on which 47 billion dollars in taxes were paid. The taxpayers assessed themselves. It is worth noting, therefore, that only about one thousand tax evasion cases are tried in federal courts annually.

It is important to understand the purposes for which force is used. Commonly governments are prepared to use great force against other governments but *not to govern their own people*.

Thus the internal relations of American government are not characteristically forceable. Internally the function of the government is to reduce very greatly the amount of force used in the management of the community; the governmental monopoly

[11] *Information Please Almanac*, New York, 1967, p. 343.

of force has the effect of denying its use to private persons. As a result very little force is used by anyone. The effect is to diminish the need for force within the community; for 99.9 percent of the people in the community force is never used at all.

Why do people obey? They obey for the same reason that the crew of a ship at sea in a storm obeys the captain. They obey because obedience is one of the conditions of survival in a dangerous world. The idea of the great need of force as a means of *governing* is an *invention of theorists who have misconceived the nature of government.* Force is a theoretical necessity to philosophers who think of government as a master-servant relation between rulers and subjects, and this in turn is a consequence of the introverted view of government.

The problem of obedience is central to the understanding of government. The traditional restricted way of looking at one government at a time compels students of government to look at the wrong set of facts, it compels them to ask the wrong question, and leads inevitably to the wrong conclusion. This approach to the problem is like trying to understand a one-man baseball game. We see a diamond, the bases, home plate, a ball, and one player. The game makes no sense until we bring in the other players.[12]

Public support for law enforcement is one of the political facts of life in the United States. When resistance to the law takes on even the slightest odor of revolution, the public becomes remarkably intolerant because the roots of the government run deep in the social structure.

The question of obedience looks different when we take an enlarged view of the situation to include the whole worldwide political system. *Government is an attitude toward the world,* a way of looking at the whole world about us. We cannot understand why people act as they do until we try to see what they see. What people see about the outside world overshadows other tensions and binds the servants and the masters together.

[12] Illusions about force have led people to suppose the dictatorships are powerful because they use large police organizations, confine many people in concentration camps, use censorship, and suppress opposition parties. Actually these measures are marks of weakness.

Since it is impossible for anyone to see the whole world physically, the only thing that we can do is to imagine it. How do we imagine the world? In the mind's eye we see what we have been taught to see, the images, the simplifications we have been brought up with. It is necessary to simplify the enormous landscape in order to see anything at all, and the greatest of the simplifications of the human world is a *map*, a map of the world. Modern man cannot think about the world without maps.

No American can think about the world without seeing, in his mind's eye a great blob of land (3.5 million square miles of it) in eastern Asia occupied by an incomprehensible number of Chinese. Or he sees another land mass extending from Poland in eastern Europe across the whole of northern Asia to the Pacific, nine million square miles of land full of Russians.

Or he sees a great pear-shaped area in southern Asia occupied by a half billion Indians, or he sees the African continent with a confused sense that he does not know where in this area he might find Uganda, Tanganyika, Zanzibar, Somalia, Togoland, Rwanda, Senegal, or Mali.

What do these images amount to? In every case these maps represent a mixture of land and people, a political map, and above all, a power system. The whole world, all of the land and all of the people in the world, are organized about the map. This is the political world. We cannot easily think about the world any other way.

We cannot help having an attitude toward the map, friendly or hostile or mixed. *A map puts us on the same planet with everybody else in the world* and divides the land and the people. By itself the land would be unimportant. It is the mixture of land and people that produces the power system.

If we could actually see 700 million Chinese or 250 million Russians or 450 million Indians and all of the other people in the world everything might be different, but we cannot do it. *Our intellectual limitations force us to use labels and simplifications.* That is why we develop the attitudes and feelings that go with the pictures we see, and the attitudes and feelings that go with the pictures have produced the tensions we call government.

The map is perhaps the most emotional invention of man. It puts everyone in the world in his place and tells everyone in the world who his friends and his enemies are, sight unseen. Everything about this habit of looking at the world *is loaded with emotion, preferences, prejudices, preconceptions, illusions, misinformation, and unproved propositions*—all related some way to the intellectual limitations of people, all built into the political organization of the world.

What is government? From the outside it looks like a security system based on the marriage of land and people. From the inside, it looks like and attempts to create a community. A government is like an oyster, hard on the outside and soft on the inside, and the outside and inside are utterly dependent on each other.

CHAPTER 2

*Why do people
make miscalculations
about government?*

It is almost inevitable that we make miscalculations about government because we start with a big, fat body of illusions about the subject. If we assume that our government is something like a private club, organized wholly for our own convenience and welfare, we are apt to get into a utopian state of mind. We begin to imagine that we can have what we want, do what we want, and build as we please, without limit.

A small difficulty about this pleasant notion is that governments are not very much like utopias. Utopians withdraw from the world to speculate about a never-never land in which they can escape from unpleasant realities as if the rest of the world did not exist. Utopias are almost the exact opposites of governments, because governments are created to cope with precisely the things that the utopians try to forget. Every government exists in a hard world full of governments prone to make great nuisances of themselves.

27

No government is ever free to do all that it wants to do. No government could possibly have the kind of relaxed, friendly relations with its neighbors that an ordinary private person might have with the people living on his street, because there is no government of governments. Governments are the most powerful organizations in the world, but they play in a big league of monster organizations.

Glorifying the past, as we sometimes do, it may seem to us that there may have been ideal states in olden times. Did the Pilgrim Fathers establish an ideal state in the Mayflower Compact? Nathaniel Morton, secretary and keeper of the records for the Plymouth Colony, did not seem to think so when he wrote in 1620 about the "hideous and desolate wilderness, full of wilde beasts and wilde men" in which the Pilgrims settled.

Nor did the authors of the United States Constitution believe that they were establishing an ideal commonwealth. Making governments is nearly always a dangerous business. The members of the Constitutional Convention were well aware of Franklin's advice given to them at the outset of the Revolution that they had better hang together or they might hang separately.

We return to the *cause* of governments. The cause of government enters into the *making* of every government; it *sustains* governments and *explains* them. Some of the more extravagant versions of the idea of popular sovereignty might lead us to imagine that the people can use their power to establish heaven on earth, but paradise is not likely to be on the ballot when the people vote.

Utopian states are by-products of the introverted view of government which considers only the inside of government and ignores the outside. Every government, as distinguished from the utopias, is torn between the contradictory demands of the good life and survival.

Nearly all of our illusions grow out of the introverted view of government. Why have anarchists never been able to abolish a government? In the face of the overwhelming pressures of a hundred governments it is impossible to do so. If a government is destroyed, another occupies its place.

The difficulties Americans have had in understanding government have existed from the beginning. Someone has said that the Constitution was written by people who did not believe in democracy, for people who did not believe in government.

In some ways it might be said that the government of the United States represents the triumph of circumstances over ideas. Americans did not intend to create the most powerful government in the world. While they were still cherishing their illusions about the lovely toy model created by the Founding Fathers, the government bourgeoned unseen, almost as if it had a life of its own.

Strange as it may seem, the government of the United States is the creation of one of the most antigovernmental civilizations in history, a monument to the ambivalence of our political attitudes. Politically we are like an overweight woman, perpetually on a diet, perpetually gaining weight. No one can understand American government who does not appreciate the capacity of Americans to live with a permanent conflict of theory and practice in which every expansion of the government is treated as a temporary exception to the principle that all government ought to be minimized.

The beginnings were almost unbelievably small. In 1792 the federal government was about as large as that of Poughkeepsie or Green Bay today. It resembled the present government in about the way Henry Ford's old bicycle repair shop resembles the modern Ford Motor Company. President Washington made his budget on a single sheet of paper. Jefferson ran his department of foreign affairs with a staff of six writing clerks. The government issued three patents in 1790. The postal service was able to get along on an appropriation of $32,000. As late as 1822 the government spent $1000 for the improvement of rivers and harbors, and President Monroe vetoed a $9000 appropriation for the repair of the Cumberland road. It takes an effort of the imagination to understand the state of mind of John Randolph, chairman of the Ways and Means Committee of the House, who launched a bitter campaign to abolish the U.S. Mint in 1801. The Mint began modestly enough by coining one-cent pieces, the first United States coin in general circulation. Randolph saw in these coins an "insignia of sovereignty."[1]

This is the grain of mustard seed from which the American Leviathan has come. Americans are extremely romantic about the miniscule origins of their institutions. They cherish the idea of a small government and want to keep it small the way some mothers want to keep their babies small.

The armed forces today are a thousand times as large as they were in 1794, the budget is 20,000 times as large, postal service is 80,000 times as large, the Mint produced five and one-half billion coins in 1964, but Americans are badly equipped by their intellectual past to understand what is going on.

This growth has taken place in spite of a structure that hobbled and handcuffed it. The fact that the government has survived and has grown powerful is due to factors not to be found in the language of the Constitution nor in the political theory behind it.

The democratic movement, in its origins, tended to be antigovernmental. Democracy began as a movement to abolish feudal monarchies and feudal aristocracies. Early democrats (Rousseau, for example) felt that the chief object was to get rid of the kings and the lords and that thereafter government would be small and simple. This is about what Marx, a century later, thought government might be like after the abolition of capitalism and the anarchists thought government might be like after the abolition of property.

That is nearly the way Jefferson felt about government. When the Federalists were thrown out of office, they too became antigovernmental. Much of the history of the American people is the story of a flight from government. The country was populated by European minorities who detested their own govern-

[1] Henry Adams, *John Randolph*, New York, 1961 (Premier Americans edition), pp. 52–53, 64.

ments. It has nearly always been popular to be against the government.

The existence of a large expanse of open country on the frontier made it possible for people to escape from organized society by going West to set up societies of their own. The geographical position of the United States fostered the notion that the American people might go on indefinitely minding their own business unmolested by the outside world.

Immigrant and religious minorities and pioneers were not alone in their hostility to government. Calhoun, theoretician of the southern slaveocracy, developed his nullification concepts when he began to realize that the slave states might lose their dominant position in the national government, and the deepening crisis over slavery tended to immobilize the national government.

After the Civil War the new northern business class developed a new body of antigovernmental ideas. Typically, William Graham Sumner used social Darwinism as the theoretical basis for an attack on government, oblivious of the fascist implications of his program for suppression of the economically unsuccessful.

Major attacks on government have often been made in the name of economy. In a little more than a century the major parties have adopted fifty economy planks. Only the flag itself has received greater support than the notion of economy in government. Economy (read the word to mean reduction in governmental activity) has been very nearly the most advocated, most avowed notion in American politics. Reading the economy planks adopted by the parties one might suppose that Americans have the smallest and cheapest government in the world.

Throughout American history, economy has been equated with virtue and spending with sin. This is the hostile intellectual environment in which the American Leviathan has grown up, the bastard offspring of antigovernmentalism and world politics.

American government has not developed the way the theorists thought that it ought to develop. No school of theorists has been able to direct its growth, not the Founding Fathers, the states' righters, the economizers, the social Darwinists, or the utopians. The contradictions are evident in all schools of opinion. The most extreme conservative antigovernmentalists tend also to be the most belligerent nationalists, innocently unaware of the fact that nothing makes a government grow like war.

The uneasiness of people about the growth of the government is related to the inadequacy of public explanations of the phenomenon. Public men have risked their necks in the process. They have been denounced as thieves, enemies of the people, spendthrifts, socialists, communists, and subverters of the Republic, as bit by bit they backed into the future amid warnings of bankruptcy, scandal, and ruin.[2]

Americans have been surprised and confused about the growth of their government because they have been watching the wrong set of facts. They have been obsessed with the introverted view of government and did not see the exterior factors that stimulate government most powerfully.

The impact of war on government is evident throughout American history.

Each war enlarged the capacity of the government to do things. Thereafter the enlarged capacity of the government turned out to be too useful to be given up.

We say that money talks? What does the budget say? Normally about 75 percent of the federal budget is spent for defense and defense related activities. The ratio of defense to nondefense expenditures holds in Republican as well as Democratic administrations, in wartime as well as peace. Congress passes defense appropriation bills by overwhelming bipartisan votes—not like other appropriations. How can we say that we know what government is, if we do not listen to what the budget says?

Defense is the biggest industry in the country. Education is second. That is what the oyster is like, hard on the outside and soft on the inside.

---

[2] The author recalls hearing President Taft say fifty years ago that he anticipated with foreboding a future Congress that might spend a billion dollars.

IMPACT OF WAR ON FEDERAL EXPENDITURES

1st peak	1814	34 million	War of 1812
2nd peak	1847	57 million	Mexican War
3rd peak	1865	1297 million	Civil War
4th peak	1899	605 million	Spanish-American War
5th peak	1919	18.5 billion	World War I
6th peak	1945	98 billion	World War II
7th peak	1964	173 billion	Vietnam War

POSTWAR EXPENDITURES

After War of 1812	Budget stabilized at twice the prewar budget
After Mexican War	Budget remained twice as large as before the war
After Civil War	About five times the prewar level
After Spanish-American War	Up about 66 percent
After World War I	Up more than 400 percent
After World War II	Up about 700 percent

The most potent stimulus to the growth of government comes from the outside, and a hundred governments can generate tensions for which there are no easily imagined physical equivalents.[3]

It is true that the government is very much more than a defense organization. It is extremely multifunctional. Nobody has ever established a government to lay a sidewalk, but once people have a government they find that it can be used to do many things. Governments pick up a multitude of assignments because as guardians of the community they have the prestige, the organization, and the resources to do things that no one else can do.

Among all of the other advantages they have, governments, unlike business corporations, do not need to make a profit. So governments are used to do most of the unprofitable work of the community. The great administrative establishment

---

[3]According to one estimate there have been 14,513 wars in the past five thousand years. (Letter dated December 6, 1967, by Andrew W. Cordier of the Fund of Education in World Order.)

developed for military purposes can be used for civil purposes, as the Army engineers were used to dig the Panama Canal. The civil functions of government expand with the defense establishment, because the general capacity of the government is enlarged every time the defense organization expands.

Thus the tensions that *make* governments also make governments grow.

It follows from the foregoing discussion that *it is impossible to understand politics until we know what government is.* The introverted view of government confuses all concepts of politics. If we misunderstand government we are likely to misconceive the whole game. The *cause* of government does not cease working once a government has been formed, and a cause potent enough to make a government is strong enough to play a role in its politics.

For the purpose of this discussion we might call the pressure of the outside world the X factor of politics. The X factor is a part of every political equation.

The theories of politics growing out of the introverted view of government neglect the role of world tensions in the formation, strength, growth, and behavior of government. Charles Beard, starting with an introverted view of government, saw no difficulty in explaining the work of the Constitutional Convention of 1787 as a successful effort of the commercial and financial interests in the country to take over the government. Beard neglected the likelihood that the hard-headed revolutionaries who organized the Convention wanted a government able to defend the new country in its infancy. The sleeper in the new constitution was the war power.

Harold D. Lasswell's famous definition of politics as "who gets what, when, and how" seems reasonable only in the introverted view of the government. It would have to be revised if we consider the kind of pressures that can be exerted on American government by the outside world. It is a one-sided view of politics to equate it with the free economic market, as Anthony Downs does, because the function of government is not very much like that of economy. The General Motors Corporation is not very much like the government of the United States. It is unthinkable that the American people would ever entrust to General Motors the power to make laws binding on the nation, to levy taxes, to administer justice, or to make war. General Motors is not the kind of organization for which men die.

The free market is subordinate to the ability of the government to defend the community. If the government fails, all market values vanish. Special interest theories of politics which explain *everything* in terms of the demands of special interest groups neglect the grandfather of all pressures, the X factor.

Politics is best understood in terms of the impact of outside pressures on internal conflict. Assuming that we are like the crew of a ship at sea in a storm, it is not too difficult to understand democracy, liberty, unity in diversity, conflict, and the resolution of conflict. The development of a community within the shelter makes democracy possible; within this framework people can disagree without destroying the social fabric because the bonds that unite them are strong. This is the basis of liberty. The X factor is the glue that holds the members of the community together, tempers the extremes of controversy, and facilitates the resolution of conflict. It makes majority rule tolerable because it gives the whole system a bias in favor of the resolution of conflict.

The government of the United States has been able to function and to grow in spite of the complexity of its formal structure because the X factor has influenced all calculations. On paper the constitutional structure looks as if there might be dozens of points at which the government could be brought to a standstill. There is nothing in the Constitution that forces the House and the Senate to agree on any bill or denies to the President the power to veto all bills or to pardon all prisoners, to refuse to make appointments to the Supreme Court, or to dismiss his cabinet officers, nor is there anything that could force the Supreme Court to hear appeals or even to sit as a court.

The system has not been used that way because the public has an overriding interest in the maintenance of a functioning government in a dangerous world. The government is full of officials who never use all of the power they have. This is a political system in which conflicts are not pursued without limit, because the outside pressures modify all calculations.

The introverted view of government leads us to suppose that government is impossible; it also leads us to conclude that politics is impossible. No one can understand politics until he looks at government in its total setting.

Nearly all attitudes toward public policy involve some concept of government. This is true of birth control and the population explosion, the Great Society, isolationism, pacifism, the communist world revolution, states' rights, anarchism, conservatism, liberalism, internationalism, individualism, democracy, the civil rights movement, the war on poverty, fascism, foreign aid, the balance of payments, unemployment, social security, open housing, urban redevelopment, national defense, communism, censorship, labor relations, the budget, the annihilation of space, the war on crime, Keynesian economics, atomic energy, foreign policy, foreign travel regulations, and liberty itself.

All involve questions about government—what it can do, what it cannot do and what it must do, what makes government possible, and what the dynamics of government are.

Everything within the government takes on a new meaning when we think of government as a *shelter organization* shielding the community within.

THE X FACTOR MODIFIES ALL INSTITUTIONS

Majority rule   Political parties
Conflict and the resolution   Pressure politics
   of conflict   Legislative procedure
Consensus   Public hearings
Force and obedience   Due process of law
Separation of powers   Democracy
Federalism   The welfare state
Complexity and delay

All are more easily understood when we take the X factor into account. All theories of politics require examination in the light of the factor that *makes* government itself possible.

What is wrong with Lasswell's definition of politics? When the crew of the ship realize that all will get into port together or all will go down together, they do not haggle about cigarettes. The point is that politics is *never* merely a question of getting something. Abraham Lincoln knew something about it when he said, "The house is on fire and I am besieged by people who want to rent apartments in it."

Public policy is a complex created by intersection of the inner and the outer demands made on the government. The conflict between domestic and foreign policy is built into the very structure of government. It has appeared as the conflict about guns and butter, as the conflict between heavy industry and consumer goods, as the conflict between the Great Society and the war in Vietnam; it arises in the crisis of the British pound, and in the controversy over the rearmament of Japan.

The introverted view of government is the cause of most of the confusion of ideas about the subject because it leads us to look at the wrong set of facts.

1. It focuses attention on the internal governmental relations exclusively.
2. It is based on a false view of the process of government formation, the origin of government, and the causes of government.
3. It results in a remarkable series of paradoxes and contradictions concerning government, the role of force in government, and the problem of obedience.
4. It leads to a misunderstanding of the dynamics of government and politics.
5. It does not explain the universalization of government.
6. It does not explain why governments have become the most powerful organizations in the world, nor does it explain the remarkable durability of the system.

7. It does not explain why there are many governments.
8. It does not solve the problem of anarchism.
9. Finally, it does not distinguish satisfactorily between the functions of government and those of nongovernmental private associations.

The greatest miscalculations we make are about democracy itself, the illusion that we might have democracy without government. The pools of quiet that grew up within the communities in the shelters have been the nurseries of democracy. Because there were many governments, there were many sources, but the hard knot of the subject is that democracy *is* a government in the fullest sense of the word and the cause of government is also the cause of democracy. People who do not know what government is are not likely to know what democracy is either, for democracy is only what the soft inside of the oyster looks like.

CHAPTER 3

Democracy
as a moral system

Democracy has no birthplace and no birthday. Nor can it be attributed to one prophet or philosopher. Its origins are as diverse as history itself, in the Greek city-states, the medieval church, the guilds, the dissident religious sects, the self-governing congregations, and the town meetings. It is a by-product of many other things. The Magna Carta was a feudal document concerned chiefly with the rights of the barons but containing some germinal democratic ideas. The Declaration of Independence was a statement of the grievances of the American colonists, including a few sentences of democratic theory. The Gettysburg Address was a funeral oration with democratic overtones and inferences. A great body of democratic assumptions has been read back into the Constitution by later generations, but no clause of the Constitution, no act of Congress, no judicial decision or presidential proclamation made the United States a democracy.

Out of the experiences and ideas of many people in many places in the course of centuries there has come a good deal of agreement about what democracy is, but nobody has a monopoly of it and the last word has not been spoken. It is still being invented and it is still hospitable to a multitude of interpretations, none final. The result of this condition is that people who like democracy have had to learn to live with a certain amount of confusion about what they believe.

The anonymity and ambiguity of the origins of American democracy suggests that the American nation itself, in its own way, made the government of the United States into a democracy in the course of its history. Democracy is not something that can be enacted by Congress or something that can be created by a governmental fiat or established by a constitutional amendment. That is not the way democracies are made. The order of events is: the nation develops a democratic outlook and begins to make democratic assumptions to fit its new attitude, and then it makes over the government, using the amplitude of resources that the people have at their disposal. Who democratized American government? The American people did it. Democracy has much to do with what people think, what they think about themselves, who they think they are, and what their attitudes are toward other people. The coming of democracy was like a change of climate. It resulted from the spread of new ideas, new ways of thinking about the relations of the people and the government, and the general acceptance of a new point of view, because *democracy is first a state of mind.*

Inevitably, there is no official democratic doctrine. In this respect it is very different from communism, which is based on a kind of holy writ and has always relied on a corpus of authoritative interpretations binding on all communists. It is profoundly characteristic of democracy that there has never been an official body able to proclaim an authoritative democratic dogma. Indeed, an official, binding dogma would itself be deeply undemocratic.

The problem is: how can we make sense out of the welter of ideas that surround the subject?

We can do something to clarify our thinking about the subject if we try to sort out two principal classes of democratic ideas: (1) those ideas dealing with the moral basis of democracy, democracy as a moral system or a state of mind, and (2) those ideas treating democracy as a form of government. Democracy is both a moral system and a form of government, and it is useful to keep the distinction in mind. It is impossible to understand democratic government until we understand the democratic assumptions. Democratic government makes very little sense until we know why people should in any case at all have anything to say about how they are governed. Unless we know why it is supremely important that people participate in their own government, the great effort required to make a democratic government work will not seem worth the pains.

It is easier to write about democracy as a moral system than it is to write about democracy as a form of government because democratic government is inevitably involved in practical questions which sometimes become complicated and confused. It is best, therefore, to begin with the ideal, not merely because that is the easy way to begin but because that is the right way, because general ideas are sharp tools for dealing with practical difficulties.

We can begin by considering democracy as *an attitude toward people*. That is how to state the basic moral proposition. Who do we think the people are? What is so important about them? To put it very bluntly, democracy is about the *love* of people. How did the great love affair of the people and the government originate? The love of people goes far beyond liberty, rights, equality, and justice. It is something positive, seeks the fullest possible self-realization; it contemplates *happiness*, overflows all differences, and creates the kind of *wealth* that can be produced only by people who enjoy their common participation in a community.

Where did this attitude toward people come from? It has something to do with our whole civilization. Some of the attitude is derived from the Judeo-Christian tradition, from the ancient Greeks, the common law, the history of western Europe, the slow growth of autonomous national political communities in the lands bordering on the Atlantic. Bits and pieces of these attitudes come down from many points in the past. Several centuries ago political ideas were apt to be expressed in theological terms, but if we look at these concepts carefully we may find that they shed light on the origins of our ideas about people. Fundamental in medieval thought was the idea that all men are equal in the eyes of God regardless of their earthly status. Medieval theologians believed in this other-wordly concept of man in spite of the harsh realities of the real feudal world all around them.[1]

The famous carvings on European cathedral doors often depicted scenes of Doomsday in which God sat in judgment on all men. The carvings sometimes showed shepherds, carpenters, and peasants ascending the heavenly stairway to eternal bliss while kings, dukes, and bishops were sent down to everlasting damnation. From the medieval idea that all men are equal in the eyes of God to the words of the Declaration of Independence that "all men are created equal" was but a step.

In the Puritan revolution in the seventeenth century similar ideas were expressed in the political-theological idea of the universal priesthood of believers. Translated into modern language, the doctrine declared that all Christian believers were priests. As priests they had access to divine inspiration equal to that of the established ecclesiastical hierarchies, thus destroying the monopoly of the established churches and tending to democratize religion because anybody might find the truth for himself.

The strong political implications of this attitude toward people is shown in Cromwell's discussions with his officers at Putney on October 25, 1647. In a debate about manhood suffrage, Ireton (Cromwell's son-in-law) declared that the right to vote should be based on property and should be restricted to those who have a permanent stake in the country. To this argument, Colonel Rainboro, one of the Levellers, replied, in the quaint language of the seventeenth century, "*Really, I think*

---

[1] "Masters and slaves are fellow men and by Grace of God may become brothers in Christ, equal before God though necessarily unequal under human law while sojourners in this earthly city." From Charles Howard McIlwain, *The Growth of Political Thought in the West*, New York, 1932, p. 161.

that the poorest he that is in England hath a life to live as the richest he."2

These political propositions were expressed in theological terms in an intensely religious age. In a secular age we express the same ideas in worldly language, but the meaning is the same. The ideas concern us because they tell us something about how we acquired the democratic attitude toward people.

Translated into modern terms, "equal in the eyes of God" does not mean that all men are equally wise or good or intelligent, any more than it means that all men are equally tall or strong. *Men are equal in the one dimension that counts: each is a human being, infinitely precious because he is human.* All else is irrelevant to democratic proposition. How can anyone better express his sense of the importance of his fellow men?

The idea of equality is important not only for what it asserts but for what it *denies*. It attacks all of the ancient structure of special privilege and says something about man himself, beyond all artificial contrived social arrangements and distinctions.

We start with an unusual view of man, going beyond his clothes, station, official rank, wealth, and schooling, beyond all of the conventional marks of status to the creature himself, to the warm, breathing, feeling, hungering, loving, hating, aspiring, living being with whom we identify ourselves. The discovery that when we get past the outer shell of custom and convention, beyond the externals, the inner person is a human being like ourselves, that all men are human, is the greatest discovery in history and the most influential idea in the modern world.

This discovery about *all* men is the basis of democratic morals. Only the compassionate are capable of understanding this truth about people. That is why there are no experts in morals: an incompassionate expert is as obtuse as an antisocial thug. Without this moral basis democracy as a form of government may be a dangerous instrument for generating destructive conflict.

2 A. D. Lindsay, *The Essentials of Democracy*, Philadelphia, 1929, p. 13.

Democracy begins as *an act of imagination about people.* For this reason democracy is a doctrine of social criticism. Because we are concerned with people as people we experience a kind of transvaluation of all social arrangements, the gross inequalities in status, prestige, and power that tend to override and oppress the little people who are easily ignored and overlooked. In the last analysis everything depends on what we think about people.

The democratic concern for people is not selective; it is not reserved for good or admirable people only. Democracy is about all kinds of people—good, bad, wise, stupid, white, black, brown, yellow, ungrateful, disorderly, lazy, the worst as well as the best. The democratic concern is for people in prison, for the poor, for the dirty, and the illiterate and ignorant as well as for the able, the virtuous, the public-spirited, the generous, and the successful. Democracy does not turn its back on anybody. It takes a lot of indiscriminate affection for people as people to run a democracy.

Democracy is a form of social criticism, not only of old social and political ideas, but of modern practice. Democracy is the great critic of monarchies, feudalism, aristocracy, dictatorships, special privilege, class distinctions, and all forms of oppression. It is also the continuing critic of existing practices: the denial of rights to racial and other minorities, the prevalence of large-scale poverty in a rich society, prejudice, and religious discrimination. It is a critic of the economy, of the law, of education, and of politics. Democracy has been the chief critic of the western world for two hundred years.

Democracy is opposed to all forms of arrogance. In democratic terms it is just as wicked to align the intelligent against the stupid as it is to array the rich against the poor or to let the successful oppress the failures. Democracy is the mortal enemy of academic snobbery and professorial arrogance. Above all, it does not array the good against the bad.

The greatest criticism of the modern world has been the democratic attitude toward people. Democracy calls for a re-evaluation of everything in terms of what it does to people, all people, the neglected people as well as the prominent people.

The democratic criticism of the world has been going on for centuries, a criticism of feudalism, tyranny, slavery, capitalism, poverty, discrimination, injustice, and oppression. It is the great critic of capitalism, but it is also the great critic of communism.

Without getting into a discussion of democracy as a form of government, it is obvious that democracy transforms the *function of government* profoundly because it is *about* something different from its predecessors. In the long history of mankind governments have been used to accomplish many different kinds of things. Governments based on class distinctions cannot help doing things that democratic governments do not do. An aristocracy is bound to support the class structure, excluding large segments of the population from power and benefits. When an army of occupation becomes a government it is very apt to act like an army of occupation. After a lapse of time an army of occupation may become a feudal aristocracy, but inevitably such a government is forced to devote itself to the maintenance of the privileges of the ruling class. A class government accentuates and deepens and perpetuates class distinctions because it cannot help doing so.

Democracy deemphasizes class distinctions and fosters the reconciliation of the classes because it stresses the common humanity of all men and transcends class distinctions. It substitutes a new set of values for the old and invites the old classes to take a new look at each other and make the greatest discovery in the world.

As a moral system democracy is an experiment in the creation of a community, the transformation of an army of occupation into a nation in which the conquerors and the conquered are reconciled by the attempt to find a common ground, displacing ancient antagonisms with new bonds of unity that could not have been understood by the masters and servants of the old order.

It is hard to realize nowadays how greatly the attitude toward people has changed in the past two centuries. Residues of the old attitude toward people can be found in the English language, in the old words left behind by the literate upper classes of predemocratic times. The ladies and gentlemen of the good old days have left us a rich legacy of contempt, a vocabulary of insults once used to express their low opinion of the people. All one has to do to find a collection of the words used by the upper classes to describe the common people in the good old days is to consult Roget's *Thesaurus* under the heading "Commonalty."[3]

low	bumpkin
vulgar	chawbacon
common herd	groundling
peasantry	boor
mob	churl
great unwashed	villain (villein)
rabble	clown
rout	hind
chaff	clod (clodhopper)
canaille	yokel
scum	hick
dregs	rube
swinish multitude	rustic
vermin	groundling
riff-raff	gaffer
plebeian	loon
mean	lout
base	guttersnipe
vile	rowdy
menial	ruffian
mobility	servile
horde	potwalloper
carle	slubberdegullion
serf	cad
kern	curmudgeon
chuff	beggar
bog-trotter	panhandler

[3] Roget, *Thesaurus of the English Language*, New York, 1937 Revision, pp. 336–337. The list is not complete.

gaberlunzie	jade
muckworm	tramp
caitiff	bum
ragamuffin	vagabond
looby	rag-picker
mudlark	cinderwench
roughneck	raffish
scrub	dunghill

Other examples of the old attitude toward the common people may be found in dictionaries published a century ago.

Walker's dictionary (1815) defines "vulgar" as "plebeian, mean, low, the common people." It defines "common" as "equal, vulgar, public, frequent, ordinary, an open ground." "Villain" is defined as "plebeian, mean, low, the common people." A mechanic, according to Walker, is someone who is "mean, servile, skilled in mechanics."[4]

As late as 1859 Worcester defined an idiot as "a private person; a common man, in distinction from one who has obtained public distinction or eminence. A rude, ignorant person; a boor; a clown; a hind; a rustic."[5]

Anyone who imagines that the Declaration of Independence and the United States Constitution established a democracy in the United States in the eighteenth century ought to consider the language of the time.

Democracy has taken a long time to come. Most of what we know about the first half-century of the Republic we get from books written by people who had a literate upper-class bias in which the period was idealized, much as antebellum southern books idealized the slave South. The common people did not write books.

What did the authors of the Constitution mean when they wrote, "We, the people of the United States"? We are reasonably sure that the expression did not include the slaves,

---

[4]John Walker, A Critical Pronouncing Dictionary and Expositor of the English Language, New York, 1815.

[5]Joseph E. Worcester, A Dictionary of the English Language, Philadelphia, 1879 (first published in 1859).

and it did not include the poor at a time when it was taken for granted that a common man was a poor man and poverty was a kind of crime.

The vocabulary of disparagement of the people has fallen into disuse or the words have taken on new meanings, have been purged of their class distinctions, or their class significance has been subordinated. Thus the *Random House Dictionary*[6] lists fifty meanings of the world "low," none of which refers to class distinctions. Other words such as "hind," "chuff," "carle," "churl," "kern," "potwalloper," and "caitiff" are treated as archaic or obsolete. Others are not listed at all. In many other instances the class stigma of the word has been relegated to a subordinate place among definitions. The identification of the word "mob" with the common people is demoted to fifth place in the list of meanings. It is only in the sixth and seventh definitions that the word "vile" refers to the poor. The fourth and fifth definitions of "boor" refer to foreign peasants. The fourth meaning of "vulgar" refers to ordinary people. Even the word "mean" refers to people of low station or rank only secondarily.

A comparison of some definitions used by the Walker and Random House dictionaries shows how the language has been democratized.

WALKER (1815)   *RANDOM HOUSE* (1966)

Vulgar

"plebeian, mean, low. The common people."	"1. characterized by ignorance of or lack of good breeding or taste: vulgar ostentation.
	2. indecent, obscene, lewd; a vulgar work; a vulgar gesture.
	3. crude; coarse; unrefined, etc.
	9. obs. the vernacular—the general public."

[6] New York, 1966.

Common

"equal, vulgar, public, frequent, ordinary, an open
ground."

"1. belonging equally to, or
shared alike by two or
more or all in question.
2. pertaining or belonging
equally to an entire
community, nation or
culture; public.
3. joint, united.
9. coarse, vulgar."

Villain

"one who held by base tenure,
a wicked wretch"["Villain" is
used as a synonym of "villein."]

"A cruelly malicious person
who is involved in
wickedness or crime."
[Distinguishes between
"villain" and "villein."]

In this way the vocabulary of indignities has been
cleaned up to make the language fit for use in a democratic
society.

On the other hand, the man in the street has appropri-
ated for his own use many of the courtesies, titles, and salutations
once reserved for the upper classes, such as: sir, esquire, ladies,
and gentlemen. Nearly everyone has forgotten that only persons
of upper class status once were addressed as Mr. and Mrs. (Mister
and Mistress).

The new attitude toward people shows itself in many
other ways. It accounts for the disappearance of blatant class
distinctions in dress. People brought up on school history books
are likely to imagine that the whole male population of the thirteen colonies was attired as resplendently as was George Washington in a Trumbull portrait. The illusion results from the fact
that the likenesses of the great gentlemen of the past have been
preserved, but who ever painted a portrait of a working man or
who now knows what a colonial farmer or artisan looked like?
Two hundred years ago it was possible to pick out a gentleman in
a crowd from afar because his whole costume was designed to
mark his status as conspicuously as possible. This was not merely

a matter of fashion. A Connecticut colonial statute ordered town constables to make note of persons who dressed beyond their station and to warn them to appear in court.[7]

What is now called the servant problem is a consequence of the changed status of ordinary people. There was no shortage of servants in the old days. Two hundred years ago London was overrun with servants. It took a squad of servants to move a gentleman from his country place to London. Footmen were everywhere, "treated like dogs by their masters" and "beaten mercilessly for very trivial faults."[8]

The deserted servant quarters of the great old houses are silent reminders of the times when there was an abundance of cooks, maids, butlers, grooms, gardeners, and scrubwomen. The servile occupations were not abolished by law; they vanished because servants became people. Even the "hired girl" of more recent times has disappeared. The emancipation of women has been a part of the same process. Women too have become people.

Poverty was once the universal condition of the common people. Equally prevalent were legal arrangements to keep the poor from getting out of hand, imprisonment for debt, for example. In fact, most prisons were at one time debtors' prisons. Poverty itself was a kind of crime, and workhouses were nearly indistinguishable from prisons. One of the first consequences of the extension of the suffrage in the United States was the abolition of imprisonment for debt.

The beauties of the Anglo-Saxon Common Law were enjoyed chiefly by the upper classes but did not mean much to ordinary people at a time when they did not even have the right to have counsel and would not have had enough money to hire a lawyer if they had had the privilege.[9]

Times have changed. Where are the aristocrats now?

Because democracy is an attitude toward people its goals are unlimited and it is never perfect or complete. It is a personal experience, a process of learning and discovery, and an expand-

[7] Albert E. Van Dusen, *Connecticut*, New York, 1961, p. 60.
[8] John Ashton, *Social Life in the Reign of Queen Anne,* London, 1919, pp. 58–59.
[9] See 6th Amendment. See U.S. Indigent Act of 1962.

ing universe. The community expands as practicing democrats learn to appreciate the humanity of the poor, of women, children, Negroes, Jews, and men of all faiths and origins.

On the other hand, there are some kinds of morals that democracy could well do without. Democracy has no place for the kind of justice implied in an eye for an eye and a tooth for a tooth. Democracy is a system for the resolution of conflict, not for vengeance. Simple black-white notions of right and wrong do not fit into democratic politics. Political controversies result from the fact that the issues are complex, and men may properly have differences of opinion about them. The most terrible of all over-simplifications is the notion that politics is a contest between good people and bad people.

Democracy is based on a profound insight into human nature, the realization that all men are sinful, all are imperfect, all are prejudiced, and none knows the whole truth. That is why we need liberty and why we have an obligation to hear all men. Liberty gives us a chance to learn from other people, to become aware of our own limitations, and to correct our bias. Even when we disagree with other people we like to think that they speak from good motives, and while we realize that all men are limited, we do not let ourselves imagine that any man is bad. Democracy is a political system for people who are not too sure that they are right.[10]

Democracy is an attitude toward people, but it is also a form of government. On the one hand democracy is a moral system, or on the other hand democratic government is a *practical matter*. What can 200 million people *do?*

[10] The second law of politics: it is impossible to get all of the S.O.B.'s into one party.

CHAPTER 4

Democracy
as a form of government

Most Americans believe in giving the people all the power they can use. Perhaps that is vaguely what people mean when they talk about popular sovereignty. The question is how much power can the people *use*? What can 200 million wonderful, confused, generous, worried, and quarrelsome Americans *do*? The difference between the theoretical powers of the people and what actually happens becomes evident as soon as we begin to look at democracy as a form of government.[1]

There have always been two principal schools of thought about the concrete shape that a democratic government ought to assume. Americans have come up with two patterns of ideas about democratic government based on two different definitions of democracy and two different notions of the role of the people in a democracy. When one asks what the people *do* in a democra-

---

[1] The following discussion is elementary because most of the confusion about democracy is about simple matters.

cy, Americans have tended to come up with not one, but two answers. This dualism is well illustrated in two of the most famous phrases in American history. Thomas Jefferson had one concept in mind when, in the Declaration of Independence, he wrote about "government by consent of the governed." There is implicit in these words an authentic American concept of the shape of democratic government.

On the other hand, in an equally famous passage in his Gettysburg Address, Abraham Lincoln spoke of "government by the people." While neither the Declaration nor the Address is an essay in political theory both have had great influence on American political thought and both have had great consequences. The role of the people contemplated in these influential statements differs profoundly.

Both definitions, government-by-consent-of-the-governed and government-by-the-people, are old; both have persisted throughout American history, and much of the confusion of ideas about democracy has resulted from the fact that the two definitions have been used interchangeably by people who seem to have been unaware of the difference.

How people define democracy is important. Since the dualism of definitions is as old as the United States itself it is reasonable to suppose that the American attempt to ride two horses at the same time has created problems that call for an explanation. Let us take these ideas one at a time.

Where did we get the idea that democracy is government by the people? We inherited it somewhat lefthandedly from no less a philosopher than Aristotle. Aristotle, who did not like democracy, did not intend to praise it when he defined it. He classified governments as (1) government by the one, (2) government by the few, and (3) government by the many. Democracy he defined as the corrupt form of the third kind. In the course of time Aristotle's definition has been twisted into its current form, as government by the people, a definition that now means something Aristotle never imagined.

It is necessary first to realize what Aristotle meant when he talked about "the many," because "the many" has commonly been translated as "the people," an expression that now means something that Aristotle probably did not intend to say. Aristotle's "many" were the free citizens of Athens, a small leisure class, less than one fourth of the population of the city. This was a privileged order, about as large as the undergraduate student body of a middle-sized American university like Yale or Princeton. Workers and slaves were excluded. Aristotle always had in mind a small government by a small upper-class fraction of a small community. He thought that the ideal state should occupy a territory no larger than one might see across and ought to include no more citizens than one might know personally. Considering the role of the classics in early American education, it is not hard to understand how Aristotle's mangled definition of democracy became axiomatic.

With some juggling, the New England town meeting could be fitted into what people supposed that Aristotle had in mind 2500 years ago. Thus Americans acquired the notion that the town meeting was the perfect form of democratic government. That is how the town meeting became the standard by which all democratic governments were judged; governments were democratic in the exact proportion in which they conformed to the model and were undemocratic to the extent that they departed from it. Thus the example of the town meeting, as romanticized in retrospect, was added to the authority of Aristotle to give us a definition of democracy.

Aristotle and the town meeting were powerfully reinforced by a Frenchman, Jean Jacques Rousseau, the great eighteenth century apostle of democracy. Rousseau never saw a New England town meeting, but he could not have been more enthusiastic about the idea if he had been born in Boston. To Rousseau democracy was government by the people in the most literal and unqualified sense of the words. To him democracy consisted simply of a meeting at which people governed about the way a cook runs his kitchen. He summed up the whole idea in a single proposition: the people meet to govern. "Among the Greeks," he wrote, "whatever the people had to do, they did themselves; they were constantly assembled in the public place."[2] A demo-

---

[2] F. W. Coker, *Readings in Political Philosophy*, New York, 1938, p. 508.

cratic government was a government by a public meeting of the whole people. "The sovereign can act only when the people are assembled."[3] He was utterly opposed to all improvements and devices, such as representation. He brushed aside the criticism that government by the people "constantly assembled in the public place" might be impossible in a large country like France by saying that people ought to be willing to make any sacrifice necessary to attend to their public duties. The public meeting of the people was nearly the only part of the government of which Rousseau approved. He disliked representatives, officials, permanent staffs, and standing armies.

More than anyone else Rousseau tried to translate the moral propositions that underlie democracy directly into a form of government without complications and with perfect contempt for all practical questions. He considered only the *why* of democracy and had no patience with the *how*. His concept of democratic government is the greatest oversimplification in the history of political thought, and his ideas have all of the charm of immediacy and simplicity. Rousseau's promise of instant democracy, something to be had for the taking *now*, must have seemed like heaven on earth to people who first heard about it. Only the utopians, the anarchists, the communists, and the evangelists have promised so much to so many.

Rousseau has been the most successful of the utopians. His writings have had a profound influence on Americans, including millions of people who have never heard of him or have never read a word of his *Social Contract*. More than anyone else he is the father of the notion of an absolute, unlimited, magical, popular sovereignty that transcends time, space, and all of the laws of physical and intellectual reality. For that reason, also, his dream about direct democracy is at the root of most of the modern disenchantment with democracy.

No one has ever seen the American people because the human eye is not able to take in the view of the four million square miles over which they are scattered. What would they look like if (ignoring all logistical difficulties) they could be

[3] Coker, p. 504.

brought together in one place? Standing shoulder to shoulder in military formation, they would occupy an area of about sixty-six square miles.

The logistical problem of bringing 200 million bodies together is trivial, however, compared with the task of bringing about a meeting of 200 million minds. Merely to shake hands with that many people would take a century. How much discussion would it take to form a common opinion? A single round of five-minute speeches would require five thousand years. If only 1 percent of those present spoke, the assembly would be forced to listen to two million speeches. People could be born, grow old, and die while they waited for the assembly to make one decision.

In other words, an all-American town meeting in Rousseau's style would be the largest, longest, and most boring and frustrating meeting imaginable. What could such a meeting produce? Total paralysis. What could it do? Nothing.

This is true not because the people are stupid but because there are too many of them. Two hundred million Aristotles would *never* get through talking. That is why we must free our minds of Rousseau's image of democracy. What would Aristotle now say if the "many" he had in mind in ancient Athens were multiplied by 25,000? A square mile of nuclear physicists could do nothing because nuclear physicists do not work in mass meetings.

If we are going to work out the problem of modern democracy we shall have to forget the old models. What can 200 million people do in an actual operational situation? It will not help us to become disillusioned about the people; it is not the fault of the people that political theorists have been stupid. The difficulty is due to numbers, sheer numbers, nothing but numbers. There is a right way and a wrong way for large numbers of people to do things. That is where we must begin. What 200 million people can do and cannot do determines the structure of modern democracy. This is a practical question, and it is dangerous to mix practical questions with theoretical illusions.

Of course, it is no reflection on the American people that the imaginary people talked about in political theory have never existed. The sovereign people talked about by the theorists is a fiction, a kind of hypothesis, like original sin, the economic man, the assumption that everybody knows the law and has money enough to hire a lawyer—unproved axioms used to buttress a whole superstructure of other ideas. Something like the sovereign people seemed to be necessary in early democratic theory. So theorists invented figures of speech and images to explain the role of the people in a democracy, an explanation that was not easy to construct because there were no precedents for it. For want of anything better the image of the upsidedown monarchy was constructed.

What the figure of the upsidedown monarchy is trying to say is that a democracy is the opposite of a monarchy. Unfortunately an upsidedown monarchy is not the opposite of a monarchy, any more than an upsidedown house is the opposite of a house.

The figure of the upsidedown monarchy does not shed much light on the role of the people in a democracy. It is possible to think of a king as the sovereign of 200 million people, but what are 200 million people sovereign of? The king? Poor king![4]

The figure of the upsidedown monarchy is trying to say something important, but it says it badly. It seems to say that 200 million people *can* do what the old tyrants once did, but that is an unreasonable proposition because the people do not do what the tyrants once did and could not do it if they wanted to.

All this loose talk about the sovereign, omnipotent, omniscient, infallible people stimulates the imagination and arouses great expectations. Taken literally, popular sovereignty sets up a nation of dictators.

Power in a democracy is collective; it is very widely shared power, and it is never unlimited. At most it adds up to control of the government, and the power available to the government is never unlimited. In terms of power the democratic proposition is a very modest one: to each individual is given a microscopic fraction of the power to control the govern-

---

[4] Perhaps Senator Huey Long's slogan, "Every man a king," was a sort of bastard offspring of the upsidedown monarchy.

ment. Each of the 200 million dictators is limited by the existence of 199,999,999 other dictators.

The people deserve a better explanation of their place and function in democracy. It is simply not practical for the people to use all of their theoretical powers.

While we are at it, we ought to get rid of confusing language such as "government by the people." Properly understood this expression is not a bad one, but in practice it is almost universally misunderstood, perhaps because people do not realize that it does not mean what it says. To say that 200 million Americans "govern" does not shed much light on the role of the people in the American political system. The function of a good working definition of democracy is to help people understand the difference between the Russian political system and the American system. When the Russians say that they have a people's democracy they are taking advantage of a bad definition of democracy to confuse the issue. Bad definitions of democracy are dangerous, as dangerous as a patch of fog on a superhighway.

The misfortune of modern man is that there are so many of him. The great population explosion has forever destroyed Rousseau's primitive democracy. We need to redefine democracy in terms of the large societies of the modern world.

It is not easy to get people to look at democracy in a practical light. The subject has been so confused by a great cloud of high-flown figures of speech, and by puffed-up language that it is difficult to get people down to earth to look at the problem. Democracy is an old word that has changed its meaning in the course of centuries. Moreover, it is one of the most emotion-charged words known to man. It has made its way into nearly all languages in the world. It is a word that is now used by many kinds of people, including many to whom the whole idea is new. Democracy is one of the most popular things on earth; an astonishing number of people want it, but the very success of the idea makes people intolerant of attempts to examine the practical aspects of democracy.

The old images and fictions still haunt old and new democratic peoples because people cannot bear to think about

POPULATION
OF THE UNITED STATES

1790	3,929,000
1822	10,268,000
1859	30,687,000
1871	40,938,000
1880	50,262,000
1888	60,496,000
1896	70,885,000
1915	100,549,000
1928	120,501,000
1946	141,389,000
1957	171,229,000
1964	190,000,000
1967	200,000,000

PROJECTIONS

1970	214,222,000
1980	259,584,000
2010	400,000,000

the gap between dreams and reality, because the old myths simplified everything, made everything seem easy, and above all because the old slogans foster a lazy way of thinking.[5]

To clarify our ideas about a working definition of democracy in a modern society we might profitably return to Jefferson's "government by consent of the governed." It is possible to fit ongoing American institutions into this definition better than they fit into the more extravagant definitions of democracy, and the role of the people in the system is more easily understood.

Once we begin to think of democracy as a practical problem we find that there really are things that a large nation *can* do. Government by consent of the governed implies the

[5] Jan Lukas, the Czechoslovak photographer and patriot, learned something about democracy during the tragic fate of his country. In an entry in his diary for September 14, 1937, the day of the death of T. G. Masaryk, he wrote, "Suddenly it was revealed that democracy is not just a gift but something to work and fight for daily." *The New York Times*, September 19, 1968.

existence of some familiar tools of popular government. One is a system of representation. Representatives are elected by the people for a limited term, at the end of which they return to the people for an extension of their mandate. This is a democratic invention that makes it possible for large numbers of people to play a role in government.

Government by consent is tied into a system for electing candidates for public office for fixed terms of office. If the people elect a sheriff for a four-year term they have made certain (1) that an election will be held every four years, and (2) they know in advance what they are going to vote about. People have an impact on government by voting for candidates; they use candidates as the tools of their consent or refusal of consent. The people do not simply vote about anything that might come up; they vote for *candidates*. These arrangements provide the occasion for popular consent.

Historically this arrangement applies to the members of governing bodies. Thus the U.S. House of Representatives consists of 435 members elected for two-year terms. For historical reasons the members of the House are called representatives, that is, the word suggests that they act for the people who elect them. Much ink has been spilled about the exact nature of the obligation of members of the House to their constituents. The speculation is idle. Art. I, Sec. 1 of the U.S. Constitution provides that once every twenty-four months members of the House sweat blood on election day. No matter how the member conceives his duty the system makes certain that once every two years he returns to the people and stands trial for his political life. This is a point at which the people get their leverage on the government. One indication of the enthusiasm of Americans for the system is that fact that they elect 800,000 public officials. Among this mass of elective officials there looms, like a mountain set in a plain, the plebiscitary presidency, the election of all elections, the greatest event in the political system, the grandfather of all elections.

The point of this discussion is that the people have a special relation with candidates on election day. Whatever else they do, *they vote for candidates*. What makes the vote important is that there are apt to be a number of candidates. The very word "candidate" means "competitor." Consent means that people have a choice. The fact that there are two or more candidates who compete for votes makes the votes valuable and it makes the election important. When people begin to think in terms of votes, elections, candidates, competition, representation, and responsibility, they are thinking of a system of government by consent of the governed.

In this system the role of the people begins to seem practical and credible; it looks like something people might be able to do.

A modern government is too large to permit election of all public officials. So the people elect the key officials, and let the government recruit the rest. For reasons that will become clear later, governments do not become more democratic by having the people elect more and more officials.

It is easy to overload the system. The people cannot elect everybody in the government, and it is impossible to hold elections every day. The candidate, election, competition, voting, representation, responsibility system is a great system, but it breaks down when it is overworked, because the people cannot vote all the time about everything.

Government by consent of the governed cannot function without some rules for deciding contests. The system is based on the certainty that there will be differences of opinion in the electorate, and there must be some kind of procedure for reaching decisions when this happens. This is true of all numerous bodies. There are a variety of rules that might be used; some make decisions easy, some make them difficult.

In a descending order of difficulty, some possible rules are:

1. A rule of unanimity—any action requires a unanimous agreement. One negative vote blocks action.
2. Action by a special majority, a two-thirds vote, for example.
3. A simple majority—approval by one or more than half of those participating.

4. A plurality—in an election the candidate who receives more votes than any of his competitors is elected even if he does not get a majority.

Which of these procedures is used is simply a practical matter. If an unanimous vote is required nothing is likely to be done. If a two-thirds vote is required, obstruction by a minority is invited. A simple majority has important practical advantages. A majority is the smallest number within any community that cannot be duplicated. It combines relatively easy action with relative stability. The practical advantages of majority rule are so great that it is likely to be used in all ongoing systems.

The practical nature of the problem is illustrated by the widespread use of *plurality elections* in the United States. Where there are a number of candidates in an election, it may be that none will win a majority of the votes. In this case the common usage *for practical reasons,* is to declare as winner the candidate receiving more votes than any other, because it is too cumbersome and burdensome to require a second election.

Practical considerations account for the widespread use of majority rule, because *an ongoing system must be able to function.* A workable rule is necessary. There comes a point in any controversy when the need to reach a decision, to *do* something, overrides other values, temporarily at least. People are able to live with these decisions because the danger to be avoided is a breakdown of the system, and all majority decisions can be revised and reversed. A surprisingly large number of decisions are tentative. The decision is to go ahead and do something subject to reconsideration as everybody learns by experience in trying to make the tentative solution work.

One of the great virtues of the American system of presidential elections is that it has *worked;* it has produced presidents who were able to hold office legitimately with public consent. A failure to elect a president (as would happen often if a two-thirds vote were required) would be a disaster that might lead to the breakdown of the regime. At this point a decision is imperatively necessary, more necessary than anything else. We can live with unanimous juries because the world will not come to an end if juries fail to agree. On the other hand, we must have a President and Congress must be able to make decisions or the government will come to an end.

Many great decisions have been made by narrow margins because we cannot always wait for a consensus. We act first and try to get a consensus later. Indeed, the worst way to get a consensus is to do nothing. It is far better to get started, to begin to move, to try something, or to experiment than to be immobilized. Government by 51 percent would be intolerable if it was going to be the final and irrevocable end of the process. (Someone has said that in the Soviet system a free discussion is permitted *until* a decision is made; thereafter no further discussion is permitted. This is *not* the American system.) We ought to look at majority rule as *an experiment in working out policy*, to look at it as a stage in a long succession of decisions. Indeed legislation is often merely a device providing for continuing the discussion. A decision by 51 percent is only the middle point in the process.

Democracy is a process for the *resolution of conflict* in which majority rule is an integral part. The end product is a consensus, but to require a consensus *before* we begin to move is to produce a stalemate.

The one thing we never say about any majority *is that it is right*. A majority has the power, and maybe the duty, to act, but it is never sanctified in democratic thought. Majority rule is no more than a practical device in a system in which no one is very sure that he is right. Since all men are imperfect and all may be wrong, the best thing is to experiment, to proceed tentatively, and give the minority the right to continue to prove that the majority is wrong.

This system makes majority decisions possible. Congress acts by voting on a motion following debate. The people vote for competing candidates in elections in which the candidate receiving a plurality wins. But no decision is irrevocable. Every election is merely one in an endless series, and no candidate is elected for life. Every act of Congress can be reversed. In 1968 we held the ninety-first congressional election, and in some old New England towns we are nearing the 200th in the series.

On the other hand, it is necessary to distinguish between the right of a minority to protest and to force continuance of the discussion and the claim of minorities to have a *veto*. Majorities can be experimental, but a minority with a veto is likely to devote itself forever to the defense of its special status.

A majority decision is a stage in the resolution of conflict. If the experiment fails, a new majority is likely to take the place of the old, but a minority with a veto is likely to isolate itself, give up the attempt to become a majority, and rely on its veto power. Under a system of majority rule majorities and minorities are fluid. Old majorities produce a consensus or they decline and are displaced by new majorities. This is what makes majority rule tolerable.

Too much fuss is made over close elections, as if there were something improper or unfair or undemocratic about winning by a small margin. In 1960 John Kennedy received 119,450 more votes than Richard Nixon. Was his victory tainted therefore? Since it was necessary to have a winner if the government were to survive, Kennedy with 50.006 percent of the vote had a better claim on the presidency than Nixon with 49.994 percent. This is true not because six one-thousandths of a percent of the electorate is important but *because a decision was necessary*. The failure to elect a president could be an unlimited disaster. For this reason we need a workable rule for deciding all elections, close elections as well as landslides.

We go further than that: in many elections where there are several candidates we accept the candidate who receives a plurality because *we need a winner*, and *no election is final*. We can live with this system because no election is forever. The losers know that terms of office are limited, and there is always another day and another election coming. The game of politics is not a one-inning baseball game. The virtue of the system lies in the endless succession of elections in which everybody sooner or later has his inning.

It is dangerous to place impossible conditions on decisions in the name of some vague concept of democracy in which everybody is supposed to get his own way. It may seem like quibbling, but many decisions, in everyday life as well as in politics, call for precision because it is often necessary to decide an issue even when the margin of difference is very small. Small differences may have great consequences in the following areas:

1. Jurisdictional lines
2. Property lines
3. International boundaries
4. Accounting, bank balances, and so forth
5. Athletic contests

We make provision for these cases because it is necessary to decide close contests so that the game can go on.

To govern, governing bodies must be able to act. They act by voting on motions following debate. The alternative here is not between unanimity and majority rule but between majority rule and dictatorship, for the shortest road from democracy to dictatorship is paralysis.

Much has been said against the idea of majority rule, but if we compare majority rule with the rule of minorities, aristocracies, monarchies, or dictatorships, it does not seem so bad. There have been some tyrannical majorities, but usually majorities have been moderate because the process of forming majorities is a moderating process. Modern dictatorships have been incomparably more tyrannical and unstable. Nowadays we have no other choice. Aristocracies are bankrupt and discredited. The surviving monarchies tend to be window dressing. Military, fascist, or communist dictatorships are oppressive.

Our system of elections, as organized by the two-party system, simplifies the alternatives of the voters. The major parties tend to limit presidential candidates to two. Is this a bad thing? A multiparty system might give us a dozen choices. Would we be better off? It is easier to pinpoint responsibility in a two-party system than in a multiparty system.

Even a multiparty system restricts the choices of voters. How many people in the U.S.A. want to be president? What would happen if we had one million presidential candidates? We would have no election at all because it is likely that no candidate would receive more than a fraction of 1 percent of the vote. In that case no one could claim to be the people's choice.

The two-party system has made presidential elections vastly more important than they could possibly have been if we had many parties. The party system boils the alternatives down to the point where people can begin to understand what the contest is about. It produces majorities automatically. That is why the Presidency, presidential elections, and the party system are the greatest creations of American democracy.

How many alternatives can a large electorate handle? How many choices ought we to have? Let's try it out.

1	a dictatorship
2	the best number
3 4 5 6	much more difficult to get good results
10	too many
100	useless and dangerous, leading to confusion and a breakdown of the system

It is nonsense to say that the system is undemocratic because the people do not have an unlimited number of alternatives. All questions referred to the people must be so defined that a large number of people can give an answer that means something. Majorities are formed by the way the questions are formulated.

Perhaps for historical reasons people have learned to participate in public life by voting for candidates for public office in the regular elections. The people express themselves primarily by voting for a man. Therefore, we are in the habit of defining public business in terms of men. We decide the most important questions in voting for men. This is what the democratic alternative looks like in practice. Many things are decided when we vote for presidential candidates, not merely a matter of personalities. We give a candidate a vote of confidence; we vote on the basis of an overall judgment about many matters but mostly about questions of confidence. It is not necessary to vote on all issues, nor is it necessary to elect all officials. A relatively small number of important officials is enough. Here as everywhere else, we do better if we keep the choices as simple as possible. The best way to further democracy is to make elections important, and elections are made important by simplifying them, by concentrating on the choice of a few important officials, not electing too many or too often, and by learning how to decide the most important questions by electing a few men.

There is a great art in using elections to produce an effective democratic system. If a public office becomes a great instrument of popular control of the government, the office itself will become so important that it attracts outstanding men. We give them our confidence and give them a chance to do their work so we can hold them responsible for the results they produce. There is wisdom in the notion that elected officials ought to have a chance to show what they can do. We do not want to be like the gardener who pulls up his seedlings every day to see how they are growing.

The American people are in the situation of a very rich man who owns so many businesses that he cannot personally run all of them. He controls them by selecting agents to act for him, giving them a great deal of latitude in their operations, but holding them responsible for the results they get.

This system of elections is a tool of government by consent because the elections are competitive, contested by many candidates. The people give their consent by making choices. These choices are made more meaningful because political competition is promoted by political parties which sponsor candidates and develop the alternatives. The opposition party is given a wide latitude to organize and agitate in an attempt to overturn the party in power. We have good reason to believe that the system works because in the course of American history there has been a turnover in the party control of the government about once a decade.

The practical strain in American democracy begins with the definition implicit in Jefferson's "government by consent of the governed." The Jeffersonian *begins with a government which governs and gets the consent of the governed* in order to continue to govern. The Jeffersonian does not wait for the people to assemble under a tree in the forest to decide to form a government. He is concerned about making an ongoing government responsible to the people. *The Jeffersonian order of events* is not like the order contemplated in the government-by-the-people formula.

TWO ORDERS OF EVENTS

I. The Government-by-the People Sequence

1. The sovereign people first decide what they want.
2. Then they impose their decisions on the government.

II. Government-by-Consent-of-the-Governed Sequence

1. The heads of the government accept responsibility for doing public business, take the initiative in making decisions, furnishing leadership, and so on.
2. Then they go to the people for approval or disapproval in an election in which they may be turned out of office.

The emphasis in the *second order of events* is on responsibility, leadership, initiative and confidence. In this political system the leadership in the government attempts to retain the confidence of the people.

The role of the people differs fundamentally in the two concepts. It is one thing for the people to govern, and it is something else *to judge the leaders of the government by the results they have achieved.* When we say that the proof of the pudding is in the eating, we mean that people who cannot make a pudding can nevertheless find out if it is good by tasting it, and if they do not like it they can fire the cook. There is nothing high-flown about this procedure, but it is a practical way of doing things, one of the great commonplaces of life. People make this kind of judgment every day of their lives, in private life as well as public.

As far as the people are concerned there is a great difference between (1) being expected to make a large number of decisions on their own initiative and then imposing them on the government and (2) being asked to approve or disapprove the work of an ongoing government. The power of the people in the second pattern might be described as the *ultimate* power, a better term than the confusing "sovereign" power. It implies that the heads of the government ought to be expected to run the government; to do the work of the government, cope with public problems, work out solutions, and carry out programs, knowing that ultimately the people will pass judgment on their work. The people do just that in the endless succession of elections.

We say that the government is responsible to the people. Responsible for what? The government is responsible for taking the initiative to do what is necessary; it is responsible for dealing with problems in advance, sometimes before the people understand them. If the government did nothing at all or did nothing until the people told it what to do it would be good for nothing. We establish governments to do the things the people cannot do. Government by consent of the governed implies that the people want a government that functions and does its job, that the people feel the need for a government and believe in government. *They do not want to do the work of the government for the government* as long as they have the *ultimate* power to judge the government and can hold the government responsible.

This gets us away from government by a continuous monster mass meeting, gives the government a job to do, and gives the people a tool they can use. This looks like a feasible division of labor between the government and the people.

Abraham Lincoln, the great saint of American democracy, illustrates the point. More than anyone else Lincoln gave currency to the idea that democracy is government *by the people*. On the other hand, the *operational theory of his own conduct of the presidency* was fully within the Jeffersonian order of events. No president ever accepted so much responsibility for doing what he thought was necessary to do, subject to later ratification by the people. He was well within the practical democratic tradition and has been well vindicated by American history.

In spite of the muddle of ideas from which we suffer, American government is today the richest, most resourceful, and most powerful government in the world; it is the great defender of the free world, the principal exponent and protagnonist of democracy, the symbol and shield of free institutions. It could not begin to play its role in the modern world if it had not long ago developed an operational concept of democracy.

Americans have developed a great body of wisdom about how to get things done. We have a saying that too many cooks spoil the broth. We say that everybody's business is nobody's business, or that no man can serve two masters. We ask, "Who's in charge here?" We have developed a whole vocabulary about public affairs, such as: hierarchy, specialization, line of command, responsibility, administration, organization, division of labor, centralization, coordination, management, delegation, leadership, program, and so on, all of which are alien to Rousseau's concepts. These words refer to large numbers making organized efforts and not to the spontaneous generations of popular sovereignty.

We need to educate the public in the use of its ultimate power of confidence and responsibility rather than to encourage it to try to do the impossible; we need to learn to respect and to use the great labor-saving tools of organized, institutionalized, responsible democracy rather than to chase Rousseau's rainbows. In this work of clarification we might make some substitutions of the elements of a working theory of democracy for primitive democratic concepts.

We might substitute:

Ultimate power for sovereign power
Government by consent of the governed for government by the people
The people shall judge for the people shall rule
Representative democracy for direct democracy
Democratic government for anarchy
Organization for chaos
Responsibility, leadership, and confidence for the attempt to force the people to do the work of the government

The figure of the court of last resort fits the capacities of the people and provides a credible function for them. It is the business of the government, the constitutional system, political organizations and leadership, and the system of elections to develop the ultimate appeal to the people. We sum it up by saying that *the people shall judge.*

The greatness of the power of the people is that they have *the last word*. The people have a right to demand that the heads of the government take the initiative to do the best job they know how to do; thereafter, the people pass judgment on their performance. What does the appeal look like? Above all it looks like a presidential election. It is the power of the people to upset the party in power if they have lost confidence in it. Sixteen times in American history the people have done that.

It is not reasonable to expect the man in the street to do the work of the diplomats, generals, economists, administrators, and lawmakers of the government any more than he can be expected to do the work of the engineers, lawyers, surgeons, technologists, scientists, managers, and so on, who work for him in private life. The common man is important in the private economy because he can dismiss his lawyer, architect, physician, contractor, and banker if he does not like the results of their work, and he is important in public life because he can overturn the party in power and get new leadership if he is dissatisfied. This is the common sense of all life, public and private, in a free society.

The ultimate power of the people to pass judgment on the government is not a perfect power but it is enough. The people cannot judge every detail of the work of the government. They can make only a general, overall judgment about the broad tendency of the government and the general results of public policy. They cannot vote every day. What this amounts to is a few large decisions on questions of general policy confirmed or reversed when they throw the party in power out or continue it in power. *But it is enough.* The greatness of the ultimate power of the people does not depend on the frequency of its use. The power works because it is there, and every public man is aware of it every waking minute of every day in his life. The whole world can be run on the basis of a few decisions every decade or so. Once every twenty-four months every congressman must return to the people to ask for a renewal of his tenure. What more do we need?

Our survival depends on a government that is able to do a vastly better job than the people themselves could ever hope to do. It makes sense to say that a diplomat (working as a part of the government) must be able to do a better job of diplomacy than the man on the street can do. A democracy needs generals who know more about fighting wars than the plain citizen does. The people require engineers who can do jobs that the average man could not hope to do. We get somewhere in our thinking when we say that *democracy is a procedure by which common men can get uncommon men to work for them without becoming slaves of the experts and technicians,* because they reserve to themselves the power to dismiss the heads of the government.

The mechanics of popular government are important and necessary, but *democracy is much more than voting and majority rule.* The involvement of the people with the government goes far beyond any kind of election. The government can function only with the daily support and cooperation of the people. The whole process of government is *about* people.

The democratic attitude toward people shows up in the very nature of public policy and in the operations of the government. Not only has democracy made over the *functions* of government, the agenda of government, but it has transformed the *way* the government works. The government depends overwhelmingly on *public cooperation.* Anyone who has observed the implementation of a new public policy—Medicare, social security, changes in the income tax, new postal rates, the annual registration of aliens, and so on, must be impressed by the efforts made by responsible public agencies to explain new policies to the public. Officials have long ago discovered that they get public cooperation when the people understand what is expected of them. The emphasis of all public administration is on eliciting the cooperation of the public.

Public *participation* in government goes far beyond voting in elections. We vote every time we pay taxes, every time we stop at a traffic light, every time we accept a social security check, every time we listen to a TV documentary or turn off the set because we object to the commercials, every time we send our children to school, every time we contribute to the Red Cross, give a Christmas present to our newsboy, pay our bills promptly, do an act of kindness, refuse to listen to evil gossip, go to work, join a union or refuse to join a union, or discuss politics at the dinner table while the children are listening.[6]

The government of the United States has survived and is able to function because *the American people want it to work.* They have a very great stake in the success of the government. The government has been able to function in spite of ramshackle structures and often in spite of confusion because the owners of the government want very much to have it work.

That is why democracy is not a spectator sport. It shows also that rights are not enough. Democracy depends on the willingness of the people to do what is necessary to keep the enterprise going. Democracy is *work.*

[6] See Paul Appleby, *Policy and Administration*, University of Alabama Press, 1949, p. 168, for a statement of many ways in which people vote.

CHAPTER 5

Why is a generation the proper period of time for the study of politics?

Everything about politics takes time. Often it takes about a generation. Dictatorships may be able to impose sudden decisions on the public, but that is not the democratic way. We are likely to feel better about American politics if we use the appropriate unit of time as a basis for our observations, because making good public policy, like making good wine, cannot be hurried. Most good things take time to make. It takes time to build a good house, to make a good road, to get a good education, to become a doctor, to grow an apple tree, to raise a good family, to work out a good law, or to develop a good democracy.

Much of the sense of frustration that people feel about the American political system is due to the fact that they take a very short-range view of the political process.

We need an adequate timetable to appreciate the process of policy formation, public consent, and cooperation in a noncoercive democracy. Consider the following:

Margaret Sanger was indicted for using the mails to circulate information about birth control in 1915. Fifty years later the government of the United States began to support a birth control program.

It took thirteen years to repeal the 18th Amendment.

The first model T Ford automobile was produced in 1909, the forerunner of mass production of automobiles. The 41,000 mile interstate highway system was started in 1956.

The high protective tariff policy of the Smoot-Hawley Tariff of 1929 was largely reversed by the Kennedy Trade Expansion Act of 1963.

In 1928 Governor Alfred Smith, the Democratic nominee for President, was defeated in a campaign in which his Catholic faith was an issue. In 1960 John Kennedy, also a member of the Catholic Church, was elected.

Social security legislation was advocated in one minor party platform in 1900 and in other minor party platforms in 1912. The federal social security system was established in 1935.

Health insurance was discussed and debated for about twenty years before the Medicare program of 1966 was adopted.

The National American Woman Suffrage Association was formed in 1890. The 19th Amendment was adopted in 1920.

The U.S. Supreme Court declared the federal income tax unconstitutional in 1894. A constitutional amendment was advocated by many people in the years following the decision. The 16th Amendment was adopted nineteen years later.

The direct popular election of senators was advocated in a long series of minor party platforms starting in 1896 and by Democratic party platforms starting in 1900. The 17th Amendment was adopted in 1913.

A comparison of President Hoover's campaign to abolish poverty in 1928 and President Johnson's "war on poverty" in 1964 shows a very great change in policies, procedures, and attitudes in the thirty-six year interval.

Experience seems to show that it takes several decades of discussion, experimentation, inquiry, and debate to put a major new policy into effect. The time consumed in the process is not wasted, however; it is a creative process in which projects are greatly improved and the execution of policies is facilitated by public cooperation as people reach a kind of consensus about the policy.

It takes time for people to change their minds. At any given moment public opinion may seem to be static or chaotic, but time changes the way people think. After a while some things seem less important or less urgent, or new interests displace old ones, or people grow accustomed to new conditions. Above all, everybody is learning something all the while.

What people think about public affairs depends to a great extent on when they were born. Since life is short and history is endless, what anybody remembers of the past illuminates only a brief segment of the whole story. The author recently asked a class of college upperclassmen when they were born—all were born in 1946, but none was able to remember much about politics before 1955. Obviously students whose political memories go back only about a decade have a staggering intellectual problem attempting to understand what is happening.

Every year death extinguishes the memories of nearly two million Americans while about four million Americans are born with no memories at all. How much obstinate, hardshell opinion is lost by this process of population replacement? How much of the way of thinking of one generation is transmitted to the next and how much is lost in the exchange? How great a body of opinion does each generation carry with it to the grave? This is nature's way of changing the world. Since people are not likely to be aware of political questions before they are ten years old, the turnover in politically conscious community is even more rapid than the change of population.

In 1965, for example,

About three-fourths of the people in the country were unable to remember Calvin Coolidge and the election of 1924.

About 130 million could not remember the great Stock Market Crash of 1929.

Only a little more than one fourth of the people in the country could remember the Armistice of November 1918.

More than half of the nation was too young to remember Hitler.

Less than one in twenty could remember the assassination of President McKinley, and only a few could remember the sinking of the battleship Maine.

More than half of the people in the United States could not remember the attack on Pearl Harbor.

There were already 50 to 60 million people who could not remember John Kennedy's election to the Presidency in 1960.

The great-great-grandchildren of the veterans of the Civil War were not able to feel as vividly as their forefathers the passions and the bitterness of that conflict.

The great-grandchildren of immigrants who came to the United States in 1910 had trouble understanding the old people's devotion to the land of their birth.

Only about 5 percent of the people in the country were able to remember the horse and buggy age.

Time refutes a million illusions. Much of resistance to change is caused by baseless fears about new people, new liberties, changes in the status of people, and changes in the distribution of wealth. Time proves that many of these fears have been groundless; old conflicts are resolved and new policies gain acceptance because people cannot help learning and changing their minds.

Democracy has not been as bad as Alexander Hamilton thought it was going to be.

The nation has not gone bankrupt because the government has grown large.

The South has survived the abolition of slavery.

Woman suffrage has not degraded women.

The world has not come to an end because the sons of workingmen go to college.

Organized labor has not taken over the country.

The income tax has not destroyed the capitalist system.

The United States Senate has not lost its standing because senators are elected by the people.

Prosperity seems to be *good* for people.

The country does not seem to be suffering because wages are higher and hours of work are shorter than they were a generation ago.

The rich seem to be doing well in spite of the income tax, government regulation, big budgets, and social security.

Money does not seem to hurt the poor any more than it hurts the rich.

Going to college does not seem to be bad for students even if they learn something about the ideas of Darwin, Freud, Marx, Ghandi, and Sorel, and find out what anarchism is.

We are beginning to suspect that nobody is going to miss poverty when we abolish it.

In spite of all social legislation, it is still true that the most highly valued status symbol in the country is a job.

Nobody regrets the passing of the sweatshops, and it is now generally agreed that the best place for children is a school, not a factory.

The revolution in agriculture, stimulated by government, has come even though the farmers resisted it.

The old farmers died off and the young ones took it
up.

Vaccination is now widely practiced in spite of early
hostility, just as fluoridation of water is coming in
spite of the same kind of opposition.

The 54 million people who die in a generation are likely
to carry away with them a large body of opinions, attitudes, and
beliefs that have not appealed very strongly to the succeeding
generation, and the new 122 million are likely to see things dif-
ferently. By the end of this century there will have been about
134 million births and 60 million deaths, making a turnover of
nearly 200 million people. Inevitably the new nation coming into
its own in the year 2000 will want to do many new things.

When people change their minds and think in new
ways, many new things become possible. We have done many
things that people once said that we should never do.

1. The Erie Canal was made in spite of James Madison's
    doubts.
2. The federal government now spends substantial sums
    of money for welfare, social security, and Medicare,
    in spite of Herbert Hoover's fears.
3. The United States has become a world power in spite
    of the isolationists.
4. Collective bargaining is now a part of the law of the
    land. We know that it has come to stay because
    school teachers, opera singers, baseball players,
    symphony orchestra musicians, and many other
    nonindustrial workers have been unionized.

By nonviolent processes we have turned the government
of the United States inside out. We developed the plebiscitary
Presidency; we stripped the Electoral College of most of its functions; we have transformed the Supreme Court; we made over
the Senate and the treaty power; we are breaking up the solid
South; we have largely abolished the old local party bosses, and
have changed the budget beyond recognition. Some of these
changes were brought about without legislation, others without
constitutional amendments, and all were accomplished without
violence.

Meanwhile, we have forgotten one-room school houses, whipping posts, primogeniture, imprisonment for debt, religious tests, the white primary, established churches, poorhouses, grandfather clauses, pest houses, open sewers, public baths, orphanages, and ditch diggers, and are about to forget poll taxes and rotten borough legislatures.

As evidence of a great change in the way Americans feel about each other, a whole vocabulary of uncomplimentary terms once used by Americans to refer to their fellow citizens has fallen into disuse. We do not now usually refer to our fellow countrymen as harps, dutchmen, hunkies, polacks, dagoes, guinies, frogs, niggers, chinks, limies, kykes, bohunks, canuks, or mickies. The change in manners reflects a profound change in the community. And what has become of the old maids?

Broadly, gradual changes, as contrasted with *events*, go on in places and in ways and in time spans not regularly watched by students of politics. The result is that great changes remain unobserved. It is wonderful to find out how much more we can see when we use an extended span of time to make our observations.

In the course of the turnover of population we have forgotten very much about the way people lived in the past. We have forgotten:

> How the past smelled, how it reeked of horse manure.
>
> How much dirty drudgery and hard physical labor there was about doing or making anything. How much hard work was done by women and children.
>
> How poor people were.
>
> How little education they had.
>
> How slow, difficult, and painful travel was. How bad the roads were and how poor the accommodations for travelers, and how few people traveled.
>
> How slowly the news got around and how little of it there was.
>
> How difficult it was to get hot water. How few people took baths. How could they live without plumbing?

How dark the streets were at night and how dark it
was indoors. How dim candlelight was.

How cold the houses were in the winter.

How short life was.

How few people read books.

How few libraries there were.

How little opportunity ordinary people had for play,
for vacations, or recreation.

How few people went to college.

How many women died in childbirth.

How many people still believed in ghosts.

Democratic government involves power, a capacity to
act, procedures for making decisions, organization, and majority
rule. These democratic processes can be best understood if we
put them in the setting of the larger unorganized movements of
opinion in the community at large. Democracy involves political
power, but it is never a naked power play. There is a time for
counting votes, but it is a great mistake to suppose that elections
and congressional votes on the passage of bills are the whole
story. The democratic process does not begin nor does it end in a
formal act. The process is essentially educational. Everything
about it is educational—freedom of speech and press, freedom of
association, competitive election campaigns, congressional
debates, public hearings, judicial proceedings, committee
reports, investigations, public accounts, presidential messages,
press conferences, editorials, controversies, protests, demonstrations, rallies, political advertisements, registration drives, pressure politics, petitions, more hearings, more debates, more
campaign publicity, more investigations, and more reports without end.

In this process everybody is going to school all of the
time and everybody is learning *something* every day. Much of
our interest in life is a by-product of this process. We tend to
overlook the educational nature of the political system because
we are obsessed with the idea that people are able to learn things
only when they go to school.

On any given day the clamor of politics may seem utterly chaotic, but that is what the learning process looks like, and over a longer period of time we are apt to find that people have learned very much. The assumption is that all men are human and all are able to learn in an open political system.

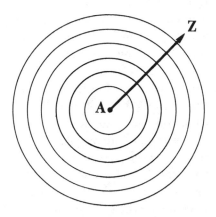

At some point in the widening circles of learning from A to Z something can be done about the problem. Nobody knows exactly how much consent is necessary. We do not need unanimity. Often we do not know when we have 51 percent or are not able to use it effectively, but the discussion is endless in this system of government by discussion.

Every statute is an experiment in learning. When Congress attempts to deal with a new problem it is likely to pass an act establishing an agency with vague powers to do something about it. The new agency makes an investigation, it issues some literature about its functions, invites comments by interested parties, assembles a library of information, tries to find some experts, tries to get people to do something about the problem, and eventually reports back to Congress, recommending some revisions of its statute. Thereafter the problem is passed back and forth between Congress, the President, the agency, interested people, the public. It is debated, criticized, reviewed, investigations are made, the statute is revised, over and over again, sometimes for years before a policy is evolved.

Often Congress and the executive agencies, more or less deliberately, keep the discussion open for a continuing discussion. Congress itself is an arena for this kind of continuing discussion, but so are the executive agencies. Nearly all labor legislation is designed to continue the debate. This is true of tariff policies, budgetary procedures, civil rights, federal-state relations, taxation, and educational policies, for example. There are very few irrevocable decisions. An examination of the grist of legislation considered by Congress shows that Congress debates the same bills over and over, year after year. Congress has already enacted five civil rights bills in a little more than a decade. How many more civil rights bills will Congress enact before we have solved that problem? In this process only the people who expect instant results fall into dispair.

How are we governed? We are governed by schools, 50 million children in schools. We are governed by the use of millions of tons of paper; by manuals. (It has been said that the Air Force issues 175,000 manuals.) We are governed by research and information. The U.S. Government Printing Office is the largest publisher in the world.

We are governed by libraries (every agency has a library of its own); by special schools for officials; by conferences of officials and the concerned public; by information services; by computers; by the U.S. Post Office, which carries about half of the world's mail; by pamphlets of instructions, such as the bulletins showing us how to make our income tax returns; by statistics; by photocopying machines.

The special character of the operations of the system is that they are public. There are a multitude of ways of finding out what is going on, and the discussion is endless. The dictatorships which lack the confidence to permit this kind of open discussion lose a tremendous opportunity to educate their people, and cut off a great source of information, an incalculable loss.

Time gives us a chance to hear the voices crying in the wilderness, the still small voices that are drowned out by the clamor of the moment.

The Greenback party in 1880 advocated an eight-hour law, the abolition of contract labor, the establishment of a federal bureau of labor and factory inspection, the abolition of child labor, a graduated income tax, the regulation of railroad rates, universal suffrage, and anti-monopoly legislation. All of these measures have become part of the law of the land in spite of the fact that the party polled only about 3 percent of the vote in the 1880 presidential election. The voice that was not heard in 1880 was heard a generation later.

The experience of the Greenback party has been duplicated by other minor parties.

PEOPLE'S PARTY
Nineteen of its 1908 proposals have been enacted into law.
Their presidential candidate polled 29,100 votes.

INDEPENDENCE PARTY
Thirty of the 36 proposals made in its 1908 platform have been enacted into law.
Their presidential candidate polled 82,872 votes.

Time proves that the race is not necessarily to the swift nor the battle to the strong. It proves that a good idea is the most important thing in the world.

Majority rule is an essential part of democracy because there comes a time when decisions must be made and we cannot wait for unanimity, but it is only a stage in the process because democracy is government by endless public discussion. We are governed by what we think. In a noncoercive civilization power is something collective imbedded in consent and consensus.

Some causes fade away because people lose interest in them, or because they become irrelevant, or because problems are solved. Nobody talks any more about the United States Bank, slavery, 54–40 or fight, the fugitive slave law, secret lodges, an overland route to the Pacific, polygamy, home rule for Ireland, free silver, Armenia, free homesteads, Chinese exclusion, the Boer war, annexation of Hawaii, Seward's folly, Cuban independence, postal savings, sweat shops, the Hague treaties, the recall of judicial decisions, the initiative, referendum and recall, the League of Nations, the prohibition of child labor, or sixteen to one, although all of these matters were once the subjects of

American politics. The discussion moves on as the business of the community is transacted.

In these continuing discussions some ideas become more influential the more they are debated, while others cannot endure an extended discussion. In the long run the result has little relation to the first reactions measured by the latest public opinion poll.

Looked at this way some old bugaboos do not look as bad as some people think they are. The separation of powers, the checks and balances, the repetitions and cumbersome procedure in Congress are irritating but they tend to kill off proposals that cannot survive a long discussion. If a cause or an idea prospers in the endless discussion, the delays caused by the complexity of the structure only give it time to grow because, in the end, we are governed by something as intangible as an idea.

When do things become possible? In a political system in which coercion is minimized, *time* and *work* are the price we pay for consent and cooperation. Government by consent is not to be understood exclusively in terms of formal public acts. The system is seen best in terms of public understandings and in the capacity of the system to resolve conflicts. Formal public enactments are a part of the long sequence, but they do not stand by themselves and are never final.

Government by consent is not automatic or instantaneous; it involves work, organization, and time. How does one get the consent of 200 million people scattered over an area of 3,628,150 square miles? It is nearly always a long story and a big job.

To a large extent, politics deals with the *results* of changes that originate outside of the political system. Where does change begin? *Anything* can start it anywhere. *Anybody* can provide the impulse. Prisoners locked in their cells, bicycle repairmen, mathematicians, refugees, tinkerers, laboratory technicians, slaves, pilgrims, the butchers who invented the assembly line, theologians, poets, novelists, travelers, monks, trial lawyers, philosophers, dead men, colonists, merchants, and teachers have set off chain reactions that have changed the world. They have used teakettles, kites, apples, wires, maps, pieces of parchment, slide rules, pamphlets, midnight oil, law suits, slogans, novels, microscopes, computers, telephones, and books.

In many instances the initiators did not intend to make over the world and often were not interested in politics at all. Perhaps this is only another way of saying that *change tends to begin in the private sector.* This may be because it is easy to start things in the private sector *because* it is private. In private life it is not necessary to persuade a multitude of people before something can be started.

The life of the nation is the source of politics. It is an error to conceive of the political system too narrowly, especially to restrict it to events taking place in the formal structures of the system. The cycle is apt to begin in the private sector because that is where almost anyone can make a beginning by himself. This is what makes private initiative so important. The private life of the community is the breeding ground of millions of initiatives; later when the chain reaction gets out of hand the government is involved.

The government waits on the enterprise, initiative, inventiveness, creativeness, and productivity of the private social and economic system, but it is equally true that the private sector would destroy itself if it could not take its unsolved problems to the government. In the natural history of change things are likely to start as private matters and develop privately for a long time before they become public.

In this sequence politics comes late. Developments become political because major changes sooner or later create problems that the initiators cannot handle. That is why politics deals with the management of the inevitable.

Politicians do not invent problems. They move in on a problem only after it has become painful. Thereafter they know how to involve large numbers of people in the matter. Sooner or later when problems get big enough they come to the government *because the government is able to do things that no one else can do.*

There is something about political problems (problems in the political stage) that makes the waiting time productive. Once a problem gets to the point where only the government is able to solve it, what does a little delay do to it? A real problem does not disappear. It gets worse and the agitation grows and grows until public action becomes possible.

Delay is inherent in the political process; it is not wasted time and it is not a time of inactivity. Projects are *improved* during the discussion. There comes a time when even the critics and the opposition contribute to the improvement and the understanding of the project. Conflict is creative because no political contest is ever fought twice on the same terms, and both sides learn something in every confrontation.

To understand why the political phase of a social problem comes late in its history, it is necessary to understand why problems become political at all. Problems move into the public arena when they get too big to be controlled privately. Politics deals with the complementary relations of the private and public sectors of the community. That tells us something about the nature of government.

The government is that agency of the community which is often best able to do things that cannot be done by anyone else, not only because government is able to do unprofitable work, but because it has a central, strategic, superior place in the community; it has the kind of prestige, authority, and resources that no private agency is permitted to have. The movement from the private to the public sector results from the essential differences between the two parts of the system. To suppose that the public and private sectors are rivals, seeking to destroy each other, is a profound misunderstanding of the system.

The succession of stages is about like this:

1. Private acts leading to a chain reaction of private activity. This leads to the
2. Creation of problems involving more and more people and
3. Unsuccessful private attempts to deal with the new problems and the
4. Recognition of need of public assistance—first attempts made perhaps by pressure groups, the most easily organized groups and the
5. Enlargement of *public* interest in the problems as:

Bills are introduced
Hearings are held
Inquiries are made
Reports are issued
Debates are held
Editorials are published
Mass meetings are held, etc.

6. When the problem becomes big enough it is picked up by the political parties and the candidates.
7. Then a new cycle of projects, hearings, debates, inquiries, reports, reviews, amendments, etc., goes on until public action is taken. Thereafter the statutes are revised, reconsidered, and amended until the conflict is resolved.

Merely to counterbalance the excessive emphasis in current literature on the decision-making process and the formal acts of government, we might consider an alternative image of American government. It is so imbedded in the nation, so surrounded by people, so involved with people—people participate in it and react to it and influence it in so many ways—that it somewhat resembles a raft floating down the Mississippi. The pilot is able to do something about steering the craft, but it does not move by its own power. It is carried along by the nation.

The most important changes are the slow changes, likely to be missed altogether by people who watch only elections, congressional votes, and public opinion polls.

It is recorded that Joshua said, "in the sight of Israel, Sun, stand thou still upon Gibeon, and thou, Moon, in the valley of Ajalon. And the sun stood still and the moon stayed. . . ."[1]

Students of politics can do better than that. They can make the whole world stand still by holding a stop watch on political movements.

[1] Joshua X, 12, 13.

CHAPTER *6*

Some political words

Ultimately we are governed by what we think. Government is a state of mind, a way of thinking, a way of seeing the world about us, something we believe about other people. Governing has much less to do with control of the bodies of people than it has with what is going on in their minds. Without some patterns of political ideas, government would be *unthinkable*.

The corollary of this proposition is that it is no more (or no less) difficult to change a government than it is for people to change their minds. To put it another way, change is likely to begin as an imperceptible shift in the way people think. An idea is invisible, intangible, weightless; it has no shape or form, cannot be poured into a bottle; it will not burn or melt or evaporate or freeze; no one can drink it or eat it or sit on it or throw it at anyone else, but *ideas govern the world*.

Once people begin to see things in a new light, everything else changes—laws, constitutions, courts, political align-ments, pressures—everything changes its relative position or weight or value or force, all equations and calculations are modified.

The question is: how do we find out about these general shifts of thinking? People are often unaware of changes in their outlook, are unable to explain them, and perhaps do not like to admit, even to themselves, that they have changed their opinions. General changes in the climate of opinion are apt to be so gradual that they are unnoticed and are not easily articulated. Moreover, people may feel that their opinions are a very private matter.

Some evidence of changes in common modes of thought may be found in the ordinary speech of people, the way people talk among themselves, unselfconsciously, when they forget themselves as they talk about their work, worries, gripes, and experiences, when strangers are not listening. That is when they give themselves away. Since people are human they cannot help talking. As they think, they talk, and talking, they do something to the language, whether they know it or not. They invent new words and twist and stretch old ones. Thus the language itself is a kind of depository of the modes of thought and points of view of the language-makers, a revealing depository, because people tell us more about themselves than they intend to.

Language is the life of the mind. Thought and language are inseparable, the work of thinking talkers and talking thinkers. Language is thus a magic mirror in which we can read the private thoughts, fears, anxieties, joys, and hopes of people long dead. We catch them in the act of making up their minds, unaware of their nakedness, telling us the most embarrassing things about themselves.

There is a wonderful candor about old words. Looking back a generation or a century we can see in their words things about the people living then that might make them blush if they realized how easily we read their minds.

Old words are a revelation of the ignorance of people, their superstitions, folly, prejudices, miscalculations, hopes, and insights. It is all there for us to see, loaded with politics. Thus, a dictionary is a political document that ought to be studied by political scientists.

A comparison of John Walker's *A Critical Pronouncing Dictionary and Expositor of the English Language*, 1815 edition, (originally published in New York in 1804) and Worcester's 1859 edition[1] proves much about the way in which the modes of thought of Americans have changed in the past two hundred years.

If we assume that Walker's dictionary is a fair record of the language used by the Founding Fathers, we may be astonished to find them using a kind of foreign language.

If the reader could by some miracle be set down in New York or Philadelphia, in the year 1800, he might be interested to find that a dollar was a Spanish coin, that a haberdasher was a pedlar, a train was something worn by women, a tire was a headdress, a bank was a mound of earth, a bumper was a drink, to clip was to embrace, commerce was intercourse, to concoct meant to digest, a cruise was a voyage in search of plunder, the word diplomatic had something to do with diplomas, escalade meant to climb a wall, a leg was that part of the lower limb between the knee and the foot, that only men had legs, that a sardine was a precious stone, and a torpedo was a fish.

If some old New York friends should happen to invite the reader to dinner he had better be there at noon. If his host offered him a canary or a sillibub, a stingo, skink, or slipslop, he would be wise to realize that he is getting a drink. He ought never to refer to a young lady as a sweater girl because a sweater, in 1800, was one who sweats. And he might be surprised to find that a warming pan was not to be found in the kitchen but in a bedroom.

If our friend became so bold as to discuss politics with his host he might be dismayed to find that the language of politics had not yet been invented. Such common political words as antisemitism, bipartisan, communism, gerrymander, socialism,

---

[1] Joseph E. Worcester, *A Dictionary of the English Language*, Philadelphia, 1859. Walker's dictionary is not a very good one by present standards, but it is perhaps even more revealing because it is not a scholarly compendium.

trade union, capitalism, lame duck, nonpartisan, sectionalism, senatorial courtesy, seniority rule, filibuster, spoils system, and straw vote are not to be found in Walker's dictionary. He would probably be well advised to keep away from politics altogether because political words have so changed their meanings since 1800 that he would almost certainly be misunderstood. Consider the sense in which Walker uses some ordinary political words.

Lobby	an opening before a room
Boss	a stud or raised work on a door frame
Cabinet	a set of drawers
Ballot	a ball
Bolter	a sieve
Partisan	a kind of pike
Candidate	a competitor
Enfranchise	to make free
Hierarchy	a sacred government
Civilian	a professor of civil law
Patronage	the donation of a benefice
Pluralist	one who holds more than one benefice
Radical	primitive
Issue	offspring
Platform	a level place before a fortification
Quorum	a bench of judges
Campaign	the time an army keeps the field
Politics	the science of government
Penitentiary	he who does penance
Electoral College	(not in Walker's dictionary)

He might begin to suspect that the Founding Fathers lived in a prepolitical age. Politics is inconceivable without speech. What could the men of 1800 think and say about politics without a vocabulary of politics? They certainly talked about politics, but they must have thought and talked in ways that are not easy for us to grasp. How great is the intellectual distance between 1800 and 1969?

The language gap runs the whole way across the board. If it is difficult to talk politics across 170 years, what about economics? Walker wipes Madison Avenue off the map when he tells us that the word advertise means "to give notice." He annihilates Wall Street by the way he defines simple words like broker, cartel, jobber, and speculate. According to Walker:

> A broker is a pimp.
> A cartel is a written agreement for the exchange of prisoners.
> A jobber is one who takes chance work.
> A manufacturer is an artificer.
> To speculate is to consider attentively.
> Industry is diligence.
> Economy is management or frugality.
> Business is employment.
> A factory is a house or district inhabited by traders in a distant country.

How would one talk to people who think that lunacy is madness influenced by the moon? Who think that the elements entering into the composition of the physical universe are fire, water, earth, and air? Who think that the stomach is the "ventricle of digestion, appetite, liking, anger, sullenness and pride?" How does one communicate with people who think that calculus is "a stone in the bladder," that empiricism is "a form of quackery," that sophistication is "adulteration," that climate is "a tract of land or air," a sophist is "a professor of philosophy," and a "Phaenomenon" is "an extraordinary appearance in the works of nature?"[2]

[2] Anyone interested in talking across a century or two may want to try his talents on some words taken from Walker: siccity, cony, sennight, alloo, afer, anility, besom, reins, shalloon, rearmouse, biggin, cully, galloway, cullion, elflock, pottle, adit, brize, candlewaster, dingle, fardle, featherdriver, gammon, gullyhole, limbeck, pinchfist, powdering tub, quern, rath, loo, barracan, bice, belowt, faulchion, refel, stithy, tuz, spatterdasher, swink, tallowchandler, taw, thumbstall, tierce, weald, wilding, and virge.

The intellectual distance that separates us from them seems to be slightly incomprehensible.

Suppose that a *New York Times* reporter and columnist could by some miracle be translated back in time to 1795 in order to interview President Washington. We can imagine the scene as the reporter enters Washington's modest office in Congress Hall in Philadelphia.

The interview begins badly because Washington thinks that a reporter is a "relater," and has never heard of a columnist. He thinks that "interview" means "in view of each other" and can not imagine what a press conference might be. Inflation is "a swelling with wind," and a balanced budget seems to be nonsense because he thinks that a budget is a bag. When the *Times* man starts to ask about the civil rights movement Washington is horrified. Later he is heard to say to Mrs. Washington, "Crazy fellow came to see me this morning. He must have been some kind of foreigner. I couldn't understand anything he said. He seemed to think that the slaves ought to have the right to vote."

Joseph E. Worcester's *A Dictionary of the English Language*, published on the eve of the Civil War, affords us another, later cross section of the new American political language.

There is a great difference between political vocabulary used by Walker and that used by Worcester. Forty years of political activity had done many things to the language. Worcester uses such words as lobby, ballot, party, partisan, candidate, radical, caucus, cabinet, plurality, administration, and electioneering in their modern sense. Governmental words such as representative, presidential elector, speaker, senator, sovereignty, state, vice president, and senator had made their way into his dictionary.

A modest development of the political language in the interval between the publication of the two dictionaries is not surprising in view of the development of the political system itself. In 1856 the nation held its eighteenth presidential election. The basic pattern of the presidential political system had been established: the two-party system, the plebiscitary presidency, the national nominating conventions, and the expansion of the electorate. (Worcester does not, however, use the word electorate to describe the voting public. He defines electorate as "the territory, jurisdiction, or dignity of an elector, as in Germany." He had no word for the collective body of American voters.). Though the national nominating conventions had been used for about two decades by the time of the publication of Worcester's dictionary, the vocabulary of the convention system, (favorite son, two-thirds rule, seconding speech, keynote speech, credentials committee, platform) is to not be found in it.

The poverty of the language of government and politics in 1859 can be understood if we remember that the subject itself, the government of the United States, was a very small affair. The federal government in 1860 was about as large as that of the city of Milwaukee is today. Its expenditures amounted to about four tenths of one percent (0.004) of the federal budget in 1967. In fact the very intensity of the conflict over slavery made it extremely difficult to use the federal government to do anything at all; only a few months later the government itself was plunged into a bloody war for its survival.

The evolution of the language of government and politics awaited the development of the subject itself. We can get some notion of the depth and scope of that transformation by examining some modern words not to be found in Worcester's dictionary. Let us take a look at a list of about five hundred political and near political words unknown to Worcester. (See Appendix, p. 123)

The list of five hundred political and politically related words is incomplete, no more than a sample used to illustrate the scope and depth of the changes in the modes of thought that have taken place since 1859. It proves that modern politics would have been unthinkable a century ago.

We can get some sense of the extent of the changes in the ways of thinking of Americans by examining the 1859 definitions of a variety of old words. The words are familiar, but their meanings and use have changed. In every case the change in the use of words reflects some sort of revolution in thought and attitudes.

antenna	"a sort of horn or hornlike process, or movable, tubular organ, on the head of certain insects and crustaceous animals."
broadcast	"to sow with the hand extended, as wheat, rye, etc."
bookmaker	"a maker of books out of other men's writings; a compiler."
career	"a race course," "a race," "a course of action," "the flight of a hawk."
commute	(no connection with commuter as we understand the word today.)
environment	"the state of being environed or surrounded.
ethnic	"heathen."
federalism	"the principles of the Federalists."
film	"a pellicile or thin skin."
fission	"a cleaving."
humanitarian	"one who believes Christ to be a mere man."
instrumentalist	"one who plays on an instrument."
jingo	"a term used in a sort of vulgar oath—by jingo."
missile	"a weapon thrown by hand or by machine."
phonograph	"to represent, print, or express by phonography." Phonography "the art of expressing the sounds of a language by characters or symbols."
poll	(many meanings)—a head, a person, a list of heads or persons, an election, a haircut, a tax, to register, to vote, the name of a parrot.
pragmatist	"a meddler."
technology	"a description of the arts; a treatise on the arts."
tranquilizer	"one who or that which tranquillizes."

relativity	"relativeness."
tractor	"an instrument of tractive power, or used in drawing." "Metallic tractors, small metallic bars or rods, invented by Dr. Perkins of Norwich, Connecticut, supposed to possess magnetic power, and to cure diseases by being drawn or rubbed over the part affected."
tuberculosis	(not in Worcester) Worcester lists tubercle, tubercled, tubercular, tuberculate, tuberculated, tuberculization, tuberculose, tuberculous, a tumor, a species of degeneration, warts, a fleshy root, etc.
anaconda	refers to a large snake, not to a copper mine.
eugenic	"an acid found in cloves."
internationalist	"an upholder of international law."
logistics	"a system of arithmetic in which numbers are expressed in the scale of sixty."

All of these words are important in the world today. In every case they refer to things today that would have been difficult or even impossible to understand a century ago. Words such as antenna, broadcast, career, environment, ethnic, film, fission, missile, technology, and relativity, are keys to the understanding of a new world created since Worcester published his dictionary. Involved in the new meanings are a revolution in communications, a vast overturn in political power in the modern world, a new attitude toward two-thirds of the human race, a new concept of the physical universe and a new attitude of people toward the world in which they live.

The missing words in the Appendix to this book are evidence of what people a century ago were *not* thinking about and what, in the absence of the ideas, the government could not do, what would have been unthinkable in the time of President Buchanan.

What is impressive about the missing words and perhaps even more impressive about the *definitions* of governmental words found in the dictionary is *Worcester's lack of interest in government.* When the subject is not ignored altogether the definitions tend to be brief, undeveloped, almost trivial, and often excessively simple. Worcester gives us an insight into an antique government, the government of another age, and into the attitudes and ideas that go with it.

There were no political scientists in 1859, and it is hard to imagine that a political scientist could have worked without the five hundred political words, or with the thin, undeveloped words that were available to him. A political scientist would have had to invent a vocabulary of his own, a tremendous undertaking, before he could open up the subject for discussion. The most common words for the description of the work of political organizations, political processes and practices did not exist, presumably because people did not *see* them, were unconscious of them, and were not curious about them, or perhaps because the processes did not exist.

Worcester's dictionary does not contain a vocabulary for international relations or the words for the involvement of the United States in world affairs. It is silent about race relations, the labor movement and urbanism, and merely touches the fringes of modern technology, the revolution in communications, and the revolution in public policy which has been going on ever since.

The general intellectual background for modern political ideas did not exist in 1859. The professional associations of the social scientists had not yet been established.

	ESTABLISHED
American Anthropological Association	1902
American Association of Criminology	1953
American Economic Association	1885
Governmental Research Association	1914
American Historical Association	1884
National Municipal League	1894
American Political Science Association	1903
American Sociological Association	1905
American Society of International Laws	1906
American Psychological Association	1892

In 1859 economists were as badly off as political scientists. Worcester defines economics as "household management" and describes an economist as "a frugal manager of domestic or public affairs." In 1859 apparently the future of economics was still undetermined; economists were still in danger of winding up among the ladies teaching sewing and cooking.

How could an economist function in a language without the word graph? Or, without words such as cost of living, standard of living, gross national product, gold standard, or business cycle? How could he get along without such words as capitalism, automation, assembly line, mass production, personnel administration, trusts, holding company, cost accounting, industrial revolution, devaluation, machine tool, manpower, or raw materials? How could an economist think in a language in which a boom is defined as "a loud noise" and depression means the "act of pressing down"?

None of the Marxian words are to be found in Worcester (capitalism, class struggle, collectivism, economic determinism, intelligentsia, monopoly capitalism, power politics, sabotage, syndicalism, world revolution, collective farm). None of the Darwinian or Freudian words are included.

The following list of words related to the labor movement are not listed in Worcester:

business agent	lock out
check off	job security
child labor	manpower
collective bargaining	minimum wage
company union	picket line
craft union	preferential shop
fair employment	secondary boycott
featherbedding	shop steward
general strike	sit down strike
industrial union	social legislation
unionism	social security
labor union	sympathy strike
living wage	unemployment

wage slave   workmen's compensation
wildcat strike   work week
working papers   yellow dog contract
work load

It is hard to imagine a labor movement without a labor vocabulary. The word *strike* is certainly one of the most exciting words in the language today, loaded with political meaning. In 1815 Walker defined it simply as "to hit with a blow, dash, make a blow, clash."

Thirty-four years later Webster lists thirty meanings of the word strike. The thirtieth and last was "strike: among workmen in manufactories *in England,* is to quit work in a body or by combination, in order to compel their employers to raise their wages."

In 1859 Worcester's twenty-first definition of strike was "to cease from work in order to extort higher wages."

In retrospect these definitions seem to belong to a remote world; it would take a library full of books to fill the gap.

The academic world was very much smaller in 1859 than it is now—a strange kind of place. Such words as seminar and graduate school are not to be found in Worcester. Ideology is defined as the "science of the mind." Individualism is described as "selfishness." Materialism "deals with matter in the upkeep and behavior of the universe." Psyche, says Worcester, is an "asteroid discovered in 1852." Neurotic was something "pertaining to the nerves." Self determination meant "determined by one's own mind." Such words as population explosion, birth control, and contraception had not yet been invented; neither had hormones and vitamins. It was a world in which a skyscraper was a sail, a motor was "he or that which moves," and a generator was "he or that which generates or produces."

Statistics concerning literacy, attendance at colleges and higher schools do not go back beyond 1870. In that year there were only 52,000 students in colleges and universities. A little less than 2 percent of young people of college age attended college. There were only 16,000 high school graduates, and only one doctor's degree was awarded. Twenty percent of the population of the country over ten years of age was illiterate. There were only eleven professors of history in the country.

Such academic words as political science or social science were unknown to Worcester, and words such as mass behavior and behaviorism would have been incomprehensible. There were no professional students of politics in 1859, and the working vocabulary for such studies did not exist. How could a student of politics function without words such as: anti-semitism, centralization, class struggle, corn belt, disadvantaged, grass roots, middle class, one-party system, populism, public opinion, share-cropper, or straw vote? How could anyone formulate a theory of politics without words such as demography, elitism, functional representation, geopolitics, intelligence quotient, interest group, mass psychology, pluralism, questionnaire, regionalism, social mobility, urbanization, or welfare state?

In 1859 people talked about the abolition of slavery, but the civil rights movement had not yet been invented, and the words without which the movement would have been unthinkable did not exist. We know that nobody talked or wrote about civil rights because the vocabulary of the movement had not yet been invented. Worcester knew nothing about words such as backlash, black belt, civil liberties, black power, color line, desegregation, Dixiecrat, white primary, equal opportunity, fair employment, open housing, tokenism, white supremacy, and racism.

The great, government-making fears that have dominated the modern world were unknown a century ago. Worcester was unfamiliar with terrible words such as:

authoritarian	concentration camp
the big lie	corporative state
black shirt	fascism
bomb shelter	fellow traveler
book burning	fifth column
brain washing	genocide
brown shirts	government-in-exile
cold war	internment camp

iron curtain   puppet state

master race   totalitarianism

police state

No force of nature since the Ice Age could have changed the country as much as it has been changed since 1859 by human thought and effort. The difference in the size, the capacities, the range of activities, and the place of the government of the United States in the time of James Buchanan and Lyndon Johnson is astronomical. These changes could not have happened without an intellectual revolution. Changes in the *meaning* of politics are involved in the great transformation because people cannot do things they cannot imagine.

Where do the new words come from? They come from everywhere. Some are figures of speech, as machine, ring, heckle. Some are derived from the place in which activities are carried on, as cabinet, house, or lobby, or from a seating arrangement, as left and right. Some come from the church: hierarchy and propaganda. Many come from military life: campaign, filibuster, insurgent, picket, and partisan. A host of political words are made by adding a new ending to an old word: anarchy becomes anarchism, isolate changes to isolationism, nation to nationalism, total to totalitarianism, and so on.

To a surprising extent political words are words invented to attack something. Of 655 "anti" words listed in the *Random House Dictionary* about half are political. (See pp. 64–68.) The political strategy of word invention often seems to be to identify something, to name it, to isolate it, and to attack it. The political vocabulary is rich in critical words.

The point of this discussion is that hardly anyone living at the time of these fabulous changes in the language and thought processes of the American people was aware of the political significance of what was going on. Perhaps our unawareness is due to the fact that we associate politics with the formal structure of the government and the formal acts of the government and do not understand very well the impact of ideas on the government.

CHAPTER 7

*Some nongovernmental thoughts
about the future
of government*

In this book we have been engaged in some speculation about the game of government, how it is played, and what it is good for. All of us are involved in the contest, more than we realize, and the stakes are high. Nearly everything we call civilization is implicated in or is a by-product of the system. No important social order, no major economic system, no moral system or legal system has ever developed outside the shelter of a government.

The assumption made in this discussion is that we need to know what government is before we can learn to use it wisely. We need to know what to expect of government, and we need to know where the outer limits of the subject are.

Since we are trying to understand government as something definite, something that can be defined, the logic of our inquiry requires us to look at the whole of it, look the whole way around it, see it from all sides, and see all dimensions of it. We can locate government in space by saying that it exists wherever man is. We can locate it in time by saying that it has a beginning. May it not also have an end?

Government is old, but it is not as old as the hills and it is not as old as man. It is several times as old as Rome, but it is not old enough to qualify as a part of the eternal order of things. In the long story of man, government is still a novelty, and because this is true, it is possible to think about its future and even to speculate about a post-governmental world.

We ought to try to get accustomed to thinking about the future of government for several reasons. Government is the most successful idea in the world, but for all its success and importance it is something imperfect. There is no ideal state. After thousands of years it is still a mixture of good and evil. The flaw in the idea is that government, the basis of the social order, is itself disorderly. About the best that can be said for government is that it solves one problem by creating another, and that therefore, we get the bitter with the sweet.

War is not the vice of a few bad governments. Of all the governments in the world only Iceland maintains no armed forces. It is not true that good governments are peaceful while bad governments are warlike. Very often governments do not have that much choice about it in a political system that produces conflict about as naturally as a cow gives milk. The governments of Belgium, the Netherlands, Denmark, Norway, Poland, Czechoslovakia, Jugoslavia, and Greece had very little choice about getting into World War II. The thing that no government can guarantee is peace.

The governments of the world are so rich and powerful and useful that it is hard to believe that there is anything they cannot do. However, if we can bring ourselves to look at the world at large, it becomes evident that the failures of the governments of the world, taken collectively, are appalling. Half of the people in the world live under conditions of great misery. Moreover, if we are going to wait for 137 governments to solve the problem, the future may be worse.

The truth is that governments are only marginally interested in world problems. They generate so much antagonism and rivalry and are so preoccupied with their own security and their parochial interests that they do not seem to have the capacity to cope with world problems.[1]

Is it not about time for us to begin to realize that a government may not be the kind of organization that can function on a world scale?

Looking at the system as a whole it is easy to see that governments now deal with unfamiliar problems. Perhaps only about one fifth of the world's governments are really stable. The territorial base of government has been greatly disturbed by the annihilation of space. Where are the effective frontiers of modern governments now? The confusion in the USA over the war in Vietnam is probably due in part to the fact that it is difficult to find the American frontier in a time in which men have circumnavigated the globe in ninety minutes. All old systems of defense have been outdated by the highspeed, long-range movement in space of unbelievably destructive weapons against which there seems to be no adequate shield. As a security system, government is not what it used to be. Even more importantly, the population explosion has greatly distorted the human base of government. These developments affect the ancient foundations of government.

It does not make much sense to assume that we can go on doing more and more of what we have been doing or that we can go on indefinitely producing bigger and bigger governments to deal with bigger and bigger problems, leading perhaps to some kind of supergovernment. Only people who are in an intellectual rut or people who have vastly unrealistic and utopian concepts of government are likely to be so imprisoned by the idea of government that they cannot imagine any other way of dealing with the future.

So far, the existing governments have blocked all attempts to set up a world government. Even if this difficulty could be overcome, a supergovernment is slightly unimaginable. Are we going to have a world-wide democracy based on one man—one vote, with a world budget and a world income tax

---

[1] In spite of the peace movement in the United States, the House on September 12, 1968, passed a $72.2 billion defense appropriation by a vote of 334 to 7.

based on ability to pay, world elections, world-wide election campaigns in four hundred languages, and perhaps world-wide primary campaigns and world nominating conventions?

The notion seems unreal because a government may be the wrong kind of organization for the job. A government is an anti-organization, an organization of a minority mobilized against the world. What would a world government be against? Would it be possible to mobilize all mankind to repel an invasion from outer space?

Most of us have our heads full of illusions about government, but the worst illusion of all is to begin to think of governments as gods. Governments do not deserve that kind of respect. Is it not time to realize that there are some problems for which there is no governmental solution?

It is dangerous to have illusions about government. It is dangerous to think of government as a cure-all for all our headaches or to try to use government as a substitute for intelligence. The mess we are in is an intellectual mess, and the way out can be found only by people who know what government is.

We need very much to know what kind of thing a government is. We might take a new look at the origins and cause of government to search for some clues to an understanding of the great governmental cycle in which we are involved. Merely as an example of nongovernmental thinking about the future of government, we could return to the tentative proposition laid down in Chapter 1, that what we now call a government originated in an ancient population explosion at the time of the introduction of farming in southeastern Asia. Since that time the population of the earth has multiplied several thousand-fold, and as population has grown so has government grown at a rising rate of acceleration. Perhaps the relation can be expressed by a rule of the thumb: every time the population of a country doubles, its government multiplies by twenty.

If a very small population explosion eight thousand years ago was enough to *cause* government, what is the present towering overgrowth of population likely to do to the political structure of the world? Everything about government is magnified by overpopulation. Every pressure and strain is intensified, inflamed, and congested by population pressure. Governments were instituted among men not because men are bad but because there are too many of them.

The chain reaction leads from overpopulation to poverty, to starvation and disease, to revolution, to pressures for *Lebensraum*, the demand for bigger and bigger governments and bigger conflicts, bigger wars, more misery, more tensions, more conflicts, more wars, and bigger governments. The first casualty of overpopulation is bound to be the brotherhood of man.

Would it not be simpler to try to cool off the political system by attacking the *cause*, by trying to check the runaway growth of population? Instead of unloading all the evil consequences of human stupidity on the governments of the world, we ought to think beyond government.

It will not be easy to control population epidemic, but it would be a thousand times as easy as it might be to create a supergovernment powerful enough to cope with the catastrophic results of overpopulation. By cooling off the political system we might gain time to work out a better way of running the world. We might get a calmer view of the problem and find out how to use the governments we now have without destroying the world.

Population control will not solve all problems, but as a substitute for supergovernment it has some important advantages.

1. It is not a form of aggression. It requires no conquests, no invasions, no annexations, no indemnities, no reparations, no armaments race, no dictatorships, no concentration camps, no alliances.
2. It involves no great redistribution of world resources.
3. It involves no imperialism, no colonies.
4. It calls for no exploitation of one nation by another.
5. It does not change the balance of power because the swollen populations of the world are not marks of strength and no power will be diminished by it.
6. It requires no world revolution.
7. It makes possible a rising standard of living for everyone.

8. All that it requires is a little common sense.

Government is likely to have a role in population limita-
tion, but it is almost shocking to realize much easier the job is
likely to be than many other things governments are now doing.
The job can be done without a great increase in public expenditures, without a great program of public works, without a great
new bureaucracy, and without force. On the contrary, population control will *diminish* government activity. We can get better
housing, better schools, and better hospitals for less money. We
are likely to have less pollution, less traffic, less noise, and less
poverty.

The unexplored political potentials of population control are tremendous, perhaps because it is the intelligent thing to
do.

APPENDIX

FIVE HUNDRED WORDS
NOT IN WORCESTER'S 1859 DICTIONARY

Anyone who will spend an hour examining this list of new words will get an insight into the scope, depth, and magnitude of the changes that have taken place in American thought in the past century.

absentee voting
absolute majority
administrative law
adult education
air war
anti-American
anti-imperialism
Anti Saloon League
anti-semitism
anti-trust law
atomic energy
apportionment
   (of representation)
Australian ballot
authoritarian
backlash
balanced budget
banana republic
big business
behaviorism
bicameralism
big lie
birth control
birth rate
bipartisan
black power
black list
blackout
black shirt
blimp

blitz
bloc
blockbuster
blue blood
blue sky law
bollweevil
bolshevism
bombshelter
book burning
border states
bossism
brain trust
brain washing
brown shirts
buffer state
business cycle
by-election
campaign fund
capitalism
capital levy
Capitol Hill
caste system
centrist
centralization
chauvinism
Christian socialism
child labor
circulation of elites
city manager
city planning

civil disobedience
civil liberties
civil rights
civil service
class struggle
closed primary
closed shop
cold war
collective farm
collective security
collectivism
colonialism
color line
comparative government
concentration camp
congressman-at-large
conflict of interest
conscientious objector
consensus
conservation
consumer goods
contract labor
cooperatives
Corn Belt
corporative state
corrupt practices law
cost of living
Cotton Belt
council manager plan
county agent
criminology
cultural anthropology
cultural lag
culture complex
culture conflict

czarism
damn yankee
Darwinism
deescalation
deficit financing
demilitarization
demobilization
demography
deportation
desegregation
devaluation
diplomatic pouch
direct action
direct primary
disadvantaged
disaster area
displaced person
division of labor
Dixiecrat
dove
draft
draft dodger
drug addict
dust bowl
economic determinism
economic warfare
ecumenism
Electoral College
elitism
Emancipation Proclamation
entrepreneur
environment
equal opportunity
ersatz
escalation

escapism
ethnic group
ethnocentrism
executive agreement
expertise
extraterritorial
Fair Deal
fair employment
fair housing
fair trade
fair trade agreement
Farmer Labor Party
farm relief
fascism
favorite son
Federal Reserve System
fellow traveler
fifth amendment
fifth column
fingerprint
flag salute
flood control
fluoridation
foreign relations
foreign service
freedom fighter
free enterprise
free silver
functional representation
gag rule
gangland
gangster
gas chamber
gas warfare
general election

genocide
geopolitics
gerontocracy
gerrymander
gestapo
G.I.
gift tax
globalism
global war
government-in-exile
grandfather clause
granger movement
grant-in-aid
grass roots
Greenback Party
gross national product
group representation
guild socialism
hammer and sickle
hatemonger
hawk
health insurance
heartland
home rule
housing
human nature
hunger strike
hyphenated America
ID card
Indiana ballot
individual liberty
Industrial Revolution
industrial union
infant industry
instrumentalism

intelligence quotient
intelligence test
interdepartmental
interest group
internationalism
internment camp
interracial
interstate commerce clause
interstate compact
iron curtain
iron law of oligarchy
isolationism
item veto
Jim Crow
jingoism
judicial review
Junker
juvenile delinquency
kaiserism
kangeroo court
Keynesianism
keynote speech
kindergarten
KKK
Know Nothing Party
Krupp
kultur kampf
labor union
laissez faire
land bank
land reform
landslide election
leatherneck
leftist
left wing

lend lease
Leninism
Levittown
life expectancy
limited monarchy
list system
literacy test
lobbying
local government
local option
lockout
lower house
Madison Avenue
Maginot line
manpower
marginal utility
Marxism
mass behavior
mass man
mass movement
mass production
mass psychology
Massachusetts ballot
master race
mechanization
media
megalopolis
metropolitan area
Mein Kampf
menshevik
merit system
metooism
middlebrow
middleclass
midterm election

migratory labor
militarism
minimum wage
minor parties
monopolistic competition
moratorium
mortality table
most favored nation clause
motivational research
multimillionaire
multiparty system
national convention
National Socialist Party
nativism
NATO
New Deal
New Economic Policy
New Frontier
news analyst
newscast
news conference
newsletter
nonaggression
nonalignment
noncombatant
nonintervention
nonpartisan
Nonpartisan League
normalcy
occupational representation
okie
old age pension
one party system
open door policy
open society

overkill
overpopulation
pacifism
panel discussion
panzer division
parcel post
parking meter
participant observer
party discipline
party organization
patronage
Pearl Harbor
penthouse
peril point
Peronist
personnel administration
picket line
plain clothes man
planned economy
planned parenthood
platform
pluralist
plurality
plutonium
pocket battleship
pocket veto
pogrom
point four
police power
police state
political machine
polling booth
pollster
popular sovereignty
population explosion

populism
postal savings
power base
power elite
power politics
power structure
Pravda
precinct captain
preferential voting
president elect
presidential primary
press agent
press conference
pressure group
pressure politics
primary election
primary group
private enterprise
profit sharing
Progressive Party
proportional representation
prosecuting attorney
protectionism
Proudhon
P.A. System
public defender
public enemy
public health
public housing
public opinion
public relations
public school
public service
public utility
pump priming

puppet state
Purple Heart
questionnaire
race suicide
racial integration
racism
racketeer
random sampling
raw materials
reactionary
red herring
referendum
refugee
regionalism
religious freedom
representative government
rightist
right wing
rural sociology
secessionist
Secret Service
sectionalism
selective service
semantics
senatorial courtesy
senior citizen
sharecropper
short ballot
single tax
smear politics
social class
social Darwinism
socialized medicine
social mobility
social psychology

social science
social security
social stratification
sociology
Soviet
special legislation
splinter group
spoils system
squatter sovereignty
stalag
standardization
standard of living
state capitalism
state university
statism
straight ticket
strategic materials
stratosphere
straw vote
subchaser
subconscious
subculture
subsistence farming
suburbanization
supergovernment
sympathy strike
syndicalism
tabloid
Taft-Hartley Act
take-home pay
talkathon
Tammany Hall
tank warfare
tax sale
tax stamp

teachers' college
teaching machine
technocracy
telecommunications
telephone book
third force
third party
time and motion study
time zone
tokenism
totalitarianism
trade association
traffic jam
traffic light
traveler's check
treasury certificate
treaty power
trench war
trial marriage
tribalism
triggerman
troubleshooter
TVA
two party system
two thirds rule
tyranny of the majority
Uncle Tomism
unearned increment
unemployment
unemployment compensa-
   tion
unfair trade practice
unicameralism
unionism
unit cost

unit rule
universal suffrage
university extension
urban renewal
urban sociology
urbanization
utopian socialism
value judgment
victorianism
vigilante
vital statistics
voter registration
wage slave
war of nerves
war zone
welfare economics
welfare state
wetback
whistle stop

white collar worker
White House
white primary
white supremacy
wildcat strike
wire entanglement
wiretap
withholding tax
working papers
work load
workmen's compensation
work week
world government
world war
yellow dog contract
yellow peril
zionism
zoning

INDEX

A

Academic words in 1859, 110, 111
Agriculture and government, 14
Alternatives, 71
Anarchists, and atheists, 4
   in Spain, 6
Anti-democratic words, 48
Antigovernmentalism in the U.S.,
   29 ff.
Anti-words, 112
Appleby, Paul, 78 n.
Aristotle, definition of democracy,
   58, 59

B

Beard, Charles, 34
Birth control and government, 119
Bolivia, 179th revolution, 7

C

Cause of government, 4
Change, and time, 84
   begins in private sector, 93
   who starts it, 92
Civil rights vocabulary in 1859,
   111
Crew of ship at sea in storm, 10,
   11

D

Democracy, as attitude toward
      people, 43
   and class distinctions, 48, 51
   consent and cooperation in, 81

Democracy (*continued*)
   as education, 88, 89
   as form of social criticism, 46
   definitions of, 57, 58, 63, 64
   and the function of
      government, 47
   in large societies, 63 ff.
   miscalculations about, 38
   no official doctrine, 42
   not a contest between good
      people and bad people, 53
   order of events in, 72, 73
   as state of mind, 42
Democratic view of human
      nature, 53
Democratization of language, 48
   ff.

E

Economics in 1859, 109
Economy in government, 31 ff.
Education, politics as, 89, 90
Elections, 65, 66
   close, 69, 70
Equality, 45

F

First law of political science, 14
Force and obedience, 11

G

Generations, turnover, 86
Government, abolition of, 6
   age of, 116, 118

Government (*continued*)
    antigovernmentalism in U.S.,
        29 ff.
    by force, 11, 17ff.
    can it solve world problems, 116
    images of, 3, 4
    introverted view of, 11
    as a minority organization, 12,
        13
    a mixture of good and evil, 116
    multifunctional, 33ff.
    and population explosion, 14,
        118 ff.
    scholarly definitions of, 7
    as state of mind, 99
    and war, 14 ff., 32 ff.
    as way of looking at the world,
        22 ff.
    why are there many, 12
Governmental processes as
    educational, 90

H–I

Hawkes, Jacquetta, 15
Images of government, 3, 4
Imprisonment for debt, 52
Introverted view of government,
    11
    as cause of confusion, 37

J

Jefferson, view of democracy, 58
Jeffersonian order of events, 72,
    73

L

Labor movement in 1859, 109
Lasswell, Harold D., 34
Legislation, as attempt to educate
    people, 89
    as way of continuing conflict
        and discussion, 90

Liberty, 53
Lincoln, view of democracy, 58,
    74

M

Majority rule, 66–68, 91
Maps, as way of seeing the world,
    23
Marxian words in 1859, 109
Master and servant concept of
    government, 10
Minor parties, accomplishment,
    90, 91
Morals and democracy, 41 ff.
Multifunctional government, 33
    ff.
Multitude of governments, 12

N

New England town meeting, 59
Numbers; what can large numbers
    do?, 60–62

O

Obedience; why do people obey?,
    22
Old fears, refuted by passage of
    time, 85–86
Oyster, outside and inside, 17

P

Parlor game, 9, 10
Plurality elections, 67
Politics; why problems become
    political, 94
    as educational process, 89, 90
    as management of the
        inevitable, 93
Political words, origin, 112
Political science, and government,
    8

Political Science (*continued*)
  in 1859, 108, 111
  first law of, 14
  pons asinorum of, 9, 17
Police, 18
Popular sovereignty, 62
Population explosion, 14, 118 ff.
Post-governmental world, 116
Public cooperation in policy
  administration, 77

R

Raft, as figure explaining
  government, 95
Rainboro, Colonel, 44
Rousseau, 59–60
Rulers and subjects, 11

S

Scholarly definitions of
  government, 7
Separation of powers, 92
Social Darwinism, 31
Strike, meaning in 1815 and 1859,
  110
Supergovernments, 117, 118

T

Time, and change, 84
  things forgotten in, 84, 87, 88

Timetable of political change, 82,
  83
Turnover of population, 83 ff.
Two-party system, 71

U

Ultimate power, 73–76
Undemocratic moral concepts, 53
Upsidedown monarchy, 62

W

War and government, 14 ff., 32
  ff., 116
Walker, John, 101 ff.
Wooley, Sir Edward, 15
Worcester, Joseph E., 101 ff.
Words, as a record, 100 ff.
  democratic substitutes for
    undemocratic, 75
  origin of political, 112

X

X factor, 34
  and politics, 35
  and revolution, 35, 36
  modifies all institutions, 36